What senior pastors are saying about this book:

Ronnie knows how to get the ball into the end zone! *10 Things Every Minister Needs to Know* is full of invaluable insight about moving your ministry team to the next level for Christ.

Dr. Tom Mullins, Senior Pastor of Christ Fellowship Church and author of *The Leadership Game* and *The Confidence Factor*

No one knows how to counsel a minister better than a seasoned minister. In his new book, *10 Things Every Minister Needs To Know Know*, Ronnie Floyd shares several nuggets of gold mined from his years of experience as a man of God and a successful pastor. This work will help any church leader to serve the Lord Jesus more faithfully and effectively. I thank God for both the book and its author!

Steve Gaines, Ph.D., Senior Pastor, Bellevue Baptist Church, Memphis, Tennessee

The world of ministry can be driven by everyone else's agenda, causing us to handle the issues of the day instead of the things of lasting importance. Dr. Floyd's book helps ministers to make the shift from living in reaction to other people's plans to living for God's. The result? Ministry is guided by a divine plan not an ambiguous guess.

Gregg Matte, Senior Pastor, Houston's First Baptist Church

Ronnie Floyd knows ministry. In fact, his 30 years of shepherding have demonstrated a unique passion and perspective on the work of Christ which can be reproduced in the lives of others who follow God's call. This book is an invaluable guide for all who desire to change the world and serve Jesus effectively.

Dr. Jack Graham, Prestonwood Church, Plano, TX

Wisdom: above all things this is the ONE thing that ministers need today if they are going to be the effective leaders they need to be. This book by Dr. Ronnie Floyd is chock full of this precious commodity. Anyone in ministry can mine TONS of golden nuggets from this mother lode of practical help that will enrich them personally and lift their game to a much higher level.

James Merritt, Senior Pastor, Cross Pointe Church, Duluth, GA

This book speaks to the heart of the matter of real leadership and it comes from the heart of a real leader. Dr. Floyd, as a seasoned leader, has emulated the truths of this book in his years of ministry. You will find it to be a must read.

Dr. Johnny Hunt, Senior Pastor, First Baptist Church, Woodstock, GA

A new book by Dr. Ronnie Floyd! Always a good read. *10 Things Every Minister Needs to Know* should be his best yet. A proven pastor with many years of experience in all areas of the ministry, Dr. Floyd shares rich insights which will be helpful to ministers of all ages. I predict a wide readership. It will be well worth the time.

Dr. Jerry Vines, Former Senior Pastor, FBC Jacksonville, FL

While serving on staff with Ronnie for eight years, one quality stands out above all others. It's Ronnie's passion to reach the world for Christ. I believe this passion is birthed out of Ronnie's early morning discipline to hear from God in his personal worship time.

John Cope, Senior Pastor, Keystone Community Fellowship

For 30 years, Ronnie Floyd has been used by God to help build churches that change lives and impact communities. The experience and wisdom he has collected over that time is now, thankfully, here for you in print to feast on. I highly recommend it.

Dr. Robert Lewis, Pastor, Fellowship Bible Church, Little Rock; Founder, Men's Fraternity

Pastors need at least three kinds of persons in their lives: a "Paul" to be mentored by; a "Barnabas" to be encouraged by; a "Timothy" to invest in. Taking this to heart, Ronnie Floyd's newest book provides a fresh resource for pastors. It crystallizes his 30 years of fruitful ministry into transferable, biblically sound principles. Welcome his wisdom and use this treasure profitably.

> Robert V. Cupp, Directional Leader, Fellowship Bible Church of
> Northwest Arkansas

The passion and focus for ministry I have always appreciated from the pastoral leadership of Dr. Floyd is now captured within the pages of this book. Biblical, timely, and relevant, every God-called servant needs to read this book!

> Brad Jurkovich, Pastor, Victory Life Baptist Church, Lubbock, Texas

Ronnie Floyd is not only a great pastor, he is also a great: • Man of God • Leader of people • Husband • Dad • Friend. While serving under his leadership on his staff team for more than five years, I learned many life lessons. Some of these lessons were caught and some were taught. In this new work, *10 Things Every Minister Needs To Know*, Ronnie describes the habits and commitments that make him who he is. I recommend this book not only to ministers, but also to leaders of all types!

> Dr. Alex Himaya, Senior Pastor, The Church At Battle Creek, Tulsa, OK

What other ministry leaders are saying about this book:

Ronnie Floyd is a pastor's pastor and a leader's leader. His new book is exactly what every pastor needs to read, absorb, and practice. He not only "tells it like it is" but also how it ought to be. Don't miss it!

> Dr. Jerry Falwell, President and Chancellor, Liberty University,
> Lynchburg, Virginia

This book is the culmination of decades of practice from one of the greatest Christian leaders alive today. The sheer beauty of the book is that these are not untested principles or theoretical suggestions. The lessons from this book were hammered out on the anvil of Christian discipleship. Dr. Ronnie Floyd is a pastor to whom I point my students as an example of godly leadership. He is a prayer warrior, and has greatly influenced me in numerous ways. I am a better Christian for having known him, and a stronger one for reading this book. Dear reader — devour this work. The chapter on prayer alone is worth ten times the price.

> Dr. Ergun M. Caner, President, Liberty Theological Seminary,
> Lynchburg, VA

He's no David Letterman, but Pastor Ronnie Floyd, not trying to be funny, makes the most of his "Top 10" list. There are other things he might have added to "his list," but if pastors would just embrace his "Top 10," their ministry would be revolutionized. Even his "Top 5" would make a world of difference.

> H.B. London Jr., Vice President, Church & Clergy, Focus on the Family

Ronnie Floyd has captured the ecstasy and the agony of ministry in these pages. He deals with the real life issues of every minister, and does so with a passion and urgency that is compelling. Every minister will be challenged to excel, inspired to serve God and his people more passionately, and greatly blessed personally by these pages. It is a must read!

> Jimmy Draper, Former President of Lifeway Christian Resources

One of America's greatest pastors and leaders has provided the matrix for all those called to be a shepherd yet called to slay giants, build the kingdom, fight battles, lead men, and still be a man after God's own heart.

> Dr. Jay Strack, President, studentleadership.net

I can't think of many tests and trials in either life or ministry that Ronnie Floyd has not faced. Without exception, he has emerged ever stronger. Reading Pastor Floyd's *10 Things Every Minister Needs to Know* is like taking the advantage of hindsight into your present circumstances. All who read it will be strengthened and encouraged for one of the toughest jobs in the world: leading the people of God forward in all circumstances.

Dr. Chuck Kelley, President, New Orleans Baptist Theological Seminary

We live in a day of rapid change. Some things must change. The church must come alive as a movement of God in our time. But some things remain vital and constant; the role of the pastor stands as a supreme example. Ronnie Floyd's inspiring words remind the reader of what Philips Brooks said long ago: "If God called you to preach, don't stoop to be a king!" Perhaps this helpful book will bring the church back to a healthy appreciation and love for the office of pastor.

Alvin L. Reid, www.alvinreid.com; Professor of Evangelism, Bailey Smith Chair of Evangelism, Associate Dean for Proclamation, Southeastern Baptist Theological Seminary

Whenever a pastor writes from the perspective of many years of success, I am always eager to observe his thoughts in behalf not only of myself but also in behalf of young ministers with whom I work. *10 Things Every Minister Needs to Know* will be a book of intense value to every apprentice minister in the country. I strongly commend the reading of this volume.

Paige Patterson, President, Southwestern Baptist Theological Seminary, Fort Worth, Texas

A preacher is dead in the water if he ever stops learning. One sure way of keeping this from happening is to stay abreast through reading. In making choices as to what you are going to read, don't miss Ronnie Floyd's *10 Things Every Minister Needs to Know*. Packed full of practical material baptized with a heavy dose of spiritual emphases, this book is a must for every person engaged in our Lord's work.

Roy J. Fish, Distinguished Professor of Evangelism, Southwestern Seminary, Fort Worth, Texas

This volume is a must read for any pastor or pastor wanna-be. Dr. Floyd has masterfully encapsulated the ten principles which will create a biblically driven and spiritually empowered ministry! The fluff is expelled and genuinely effective substance is emphasized!

Dr. Phil Roberts, President, Midwestern Baptist Theological Seminary

One of the greatest things a minister can do is to be a lifelong learner. While seminars and studies greatly aid the minister, experience is unparalleled as a teacher. Dr. Floyd has faithfully served for 30 years and an incredible 20 years in one church. The experiences of this man are now being shared in a clear way for all who desire to be faithful ministers. I commend Ronnie for helping us by sharing himself.

Rex M. Horne, Jr., President, Ouachita Baptist University

When a pastor like Ronnie Floyd speaks, I listen — and so should every pastor. After 20 years pastoring the same church, he is a pastor's pastor, and this book reads like the sage advice of Paul to Timothy. It will be a great gift to the church and her leaders and I only wish I had read it years ago.

Dr. Ed Stetzer, Missiologist and Senior Director, NAMB

I don't know of anyone who could better write this book to young pastors than Ronnie Floyd. He has successfully served in all sizes of churches and in all types of locations. Every pastor should read this book, and every deacon should buy one for his pastor.

Elmer Towns, Dean, School of Religion, Liberty University

In an era when pastors have principles without practice and truth without tactics, Dr. Ronnie Floyd has combined biblical balance and godly wisdom for ministers from all walks of life. If you desire to save years of having to learn life's hardest lessons alone, then *10 Things Every Minister Needs To Know* is a must for you.

> Dr. James O. Davis, Cofounder/President/CEO, Global Pastors
> Network, Orlando, Florida

Having served with Dr. Floyd as his second man, I know that this book reflects a heart to coach and invest in every minister with a teachable spirit. You will resonate with his insights and practical applications no matter where you minister or in what capacity. *10 Things Every Minister Needs To Know* should be required discussion on every staff team and in every seminary classroom.

> Rick Ray, Founder, Sec2ndman Ministries,
> www.sec2ndman.com

It has been my joy to serve alongside pastor Ronnie Floyd for almost 18 years. We have conducted thousands of services together in all kinds of environments. He is the real thing . . . a man after God's own heart. Ronnie Floyd loves pastors and church staff. His life is characterized by his concern for the next generation of leaders. In this practical and profound new book, *10 Things Every Minister Needs to Know,* Ronnie Floyd gives real life, everyday insight into what it takes to be a successful servant leader. I have witnessed these principles in action, and they result in spiritual health and visionary growth. If you want to stay out of the ditches of ministry and stay on the road to success and joy in ministry, this book is a must read.

> Buster Pray, Founder & President, PureChurch Consulting

As a pastor and friend, Dr. Ronnie Floyd shares his heart in a real and transparent way. He issues a call for all of us to passionately pursue God, focus on the majors, and never neglect God's people or our own lives. Every pastor and ministry leader will have an immediate life change if they apply these ten things.

> Brad Graves, Director of Church Launching, Cleveland Hope

What other ministers are saying about this book:

Spiritual leadership with passion, excellence, and consistency is what I have personally experienced. For ten years I have watched, served, and witnessed Ronnie Floyd put these ten secrets into action. This book will help you maximize your life for God's glory. I truly believe this is the handbook for successful ministry.

> Drew Tucker, Associate Pastor/Campus Coordinator, The Church at
> Pinnacle Hills, Rogers, Arkansas

You need to read this! 100% practical, completely applicable and straight to the point, Dr. Floyd has written 2006's "must read" for ministers — whether you are at the starting point or looking to finish strong. One of God's greatest blessings to me is that I have the privilege of watching these principles lived out every day. Don't just read it . . . make these ten things soar in your life!

> Jeff Young, Associate Pastor/Campus Coordinator, First Baptist Church
> of Springdale, Arkansas

Ronnie Floyd has given his life eating, sleeping, and breathing ministry. His years of serving Jesus and His church have given him insights that are biblical, practical, meaningful, and powerful! I couldn't put this book down. If you want your iron sharpened, then allow the iron of this book to whet your ministry edge. These ten principles will make a difference in you so you can make a difference in your ministry!

> Allan Taylor, Minister of Education, First Baptist Church, Woodstock,
> Georgia

10

THINGS

EVERY MINISTER
NEEDS TO
KNOW

~§§§~

RONNIE FLOYD

FOREWORD BY DR. EDWIN YOUNG

First printing: August 2006
Second printing: March 2007

ISBN-13: 978-0-89221-655-0
ISBN-10: 0-89221-655-7
Library of Congress Number: 2006929480

Cover by Brent Spurlock

All Scripture is from the Holman Christian Standard Bible unless otherwise noted.

Printed in the United States of America

For information regarding author interviews, please contact the publicity department at (870) 438-5288.

Please visit our website for other great titles:
www.newleafpress.net

New Leaf Press
A Division of New Leaf Publishing Group

I WANT TO THANK

JESUS CHRIST: for changing my life and calling me into this world of ministry. I love it! What a great life.

MY MOM AND DAD: for raising me in a small membership church, and having ministers in our home continually. Dad went to see Jesus on November 17, 2005, while sitting in his chair . . . we all miss him so much. Mom is making it daily, moment-by-moment, by God's grace, and still connected to her church.

FRED AND EFFIE THOMAS: for serving Christ for over 50 years as a pastor, before the Lord called Fred home some years ago. Fred and Effie raised my wife, Jeana, in the home of a pastor. She always told her dad, "I will never marry a pastor!" Fred always laughed at that after Jeana and I married, having joked with me about it for years, even stating, "Some say you didn't marry a pastor!" Effie is still engaged in her church.

MY FAMILY: for serving Christ with me all of these years. To Jeana, we will be married for 30 years on December 31, 2006. I love you and I am so glad you have stood with me all of these years in ministry. It has been a joy to do ministry with you, living the same life, not you having a life and me having a life. To Josh and Kate, you model what ministers love by being committed to Jesus, marriage, and family, and yes, His precious church and commission to make disciples. To Nick and Meredith, you are special servants of the Lord and your ministry life is unlimited.

PEYTON: for the joy you have brought to our family as our first grandchild. Remember, when your "Pops" held you from the moment you were born and following, he has always told you two things. "Peyton, remember Pops loves you and be sure you change your generation!"

ANITA STEWART: for taking my initial manuscript and doing the first edit on it before it went to the publisher. Your ministry heart always comes through in everything you do.

MELISSA SWAIN: for securing the various endorsements and other details to help us with this project.

MY CHURCH: for loving and supporting me 24/7, modeling before the world what a great pastor-church relationship should be, as well as being one of the greatest and most outstanding churches in the world for your Great Commission heart . . . you truly demonstrate missional relevance and orthodoxy packaged in innovation.

MY STAFF TEAM: for being a family to one another and me. Remember, who you do ministry with in life is far more important than where you do it. You are a joy!

THE MINISTERS WHO HAVE COME THROUGH OUR MINISTRY: for those of you called by God, under our leadership, or who have served with me and given me the privilege to put my life into you . . . change the world!

THE MINISTERS WHO READ THIS BOOK: for changing the world!

MY PUBLISHER: for publishing a book for ministers of which most publishers will not do. Your investment in this project will result in God doing some great things in the world, far beyond our lifetimes!

DEAR FRIEND AND CO-LABORER IN MINISTRY,

I TRUST AND PRAY THAT THE TESTED PRINCIPLES CONTAINED IN THIS BOOK WILL BLESS YOUR MINISTRY AND LIFE. AS LEADERS OF THE CHURCH, GOD'S CALLING AND COVERING ON OUR LIVES COME WITH A PRICE — OBEDIENCE AND SERVANTHOOD.

YOU MAY FIND ADDITIONAL FAITH-STRENGTHENING RESOURCES BY VISITING MY WEBSITE AT WWW.RONNIEFLOYD.COM. THERE YOU WILL FIND PAST MESSAGES AND OTHER HELPFUL RESOURCES AS WELL AS MY BLOG, BETWEEN SUNDAYS.

CONTENTS

FOREWORD

RONNIE FLOYD HAS WRITTEN a book beneficial for ministers of every generation. Older ministers will think, *I wish I'd read this 25 years ago,* but they will also find the principles Dr. Floyd details helpful in their present circumstances. Men in the middle of their career sometimes wrestle with burnout. God will use Dr. Floyd's insights to re-ignite the flame for "men in the middle." Young ministers will gain invaluable understanding of the practicalities of daily living as a minister. Dr. Floyd provides concepts that will guide an entire career. In three decades of ministry, Dr. Floyd has not lost his ideals, and shows how to balance idealism and realism.

Dr. Floyd's love for his "world" is infectious. "Reflecting upon my 30 years as a pastor of a local church makes me want to go back and do it again," he writes. Rather than seeing the demands as daily drudgery, Dr. Floyd presents ministry as an "adventure."

One of Dr. Floyd's indispensable insights is in the phrase he uses several times, "the world of ministry." Compartmentalization results in a minister regarding himself one way in the "church world" and another in the "secular world." This leads to inconsistency of witness, and sometimes even moral failure, as a man separates his character from his calling.

Dr. Floyd reminds us that ministry isn't something we do, but a world we inhabit. Understanding reality this way enables us to see actions and relationships as part of that world, and order them accordingly.

Ronnie Floyd does not write from remote, untouchable heights. This is a man in the trenches of everyday ministry. The "Top 10 Things" derive not from academic preoccupation — though Ronnie Floyd is a top-flight scholar — but from, as he puts it, "my ministry journey."

Dr. Floyd considers himself, like Paul, a debtor to many — "farmers, ranchers, private business owners, housewives, educators, entrepreneurs, politicians, lawyers, doctors, technicians, engineers, refinery workers, junior executives, coaches, executives, presidents, fishermen, chief executive officers, economists, chairmen of boards, and many others."

Dr. Floyd is honest. He hasn't written a fairy tale, but a factual account. "In this world of ministry, I can go from the top of Mount Everest to the bottom of the ocean all within just a matter of minutes," he says.

The tone of the book is inspiring throughout. Though Dr. Floyd hasn't always found ministry to be "fun," he still says, "There's nothing like it in the world."

As one who has spent decades in local church ministry, I can respond with a solid "Amen!"

— Ed Young

INTRODUCTION

THERE IS NOTHING LIKE IT in the world. I did not sign up for it nor was I recruited to do it. I was drafted by the owner when I was only 16 years old.

He discovered me, drafted me, and signed me to it from the heart of small church America. When I say small, I mean small. If 40 people were there on Sunday mornings, it was a big day. If you showed up and wanted to sing a solo, you were on! American Idol had nothing on my church. If a time for testimonies occurred, you had better be ready. If need be, push rewind and repeat. If you went to sleep while the pastor was giving his message for the day, he might wake you up. Yes, one day he called my name out in front of the whole church: "Ronnie, you need to wake up while I am preaching!" Guess what? I have not gone to sleep in church since I was a little boy. You probably did not believe me, but I told you it was small.

When God drafted me into the world of ministry, He risked so much. As I reflect, knowing what I know today, I am amazed

He wanted me to be on His team. Only five months before, He had drafted me to be a part of His family. Even though my parents took me to church at least three times a week, for some reason I did not get it. Finally, I entered into that personal relationship with Jesus Christ.

Football was my life. I wanted to play as much as I could for as long as possible. After that, I wanted to be a football coach more than anything in the world.

When God began to change my personal agenda, He did it radically. When I settled that He had indeed called me into ministry, I almost raced down the aisle of that small membership church. On that Sunday morning in March, I entered the world of ministry.

There is nothing like it in the world. At the age of 20 years, I began to pastor a church on the weekends. Ironically, if we had 50 people in attendance on any Sunday, you would have thought spiritual awakening had permeated that town of 300 people.

Since entering the world of ministry, I am serving my fifth church as a pastor. I understand your world.

The size of your church or even the size of your town does not matter nearly as much as you might think. What matters most is whether you are being all God intends you to be where you are. God wants you to not only be faithful, but fruitful.

Where you serve and whom you serve as a minister may change. The most important thing is that you change. So many ministers think, *If I could just go here or I could just do that, I would be so much better and could do so much more.*

Changing locations does not guarantee the change that may need to take place.

Becoming better at what you do and doing more with what you have is between you and God. Where you are located and whom you serve as a minister rarely enters into this dynamic.

Reflecting upon my 30 years as a pastor of a local church makes me want to go back and do it again. Yes, I was drafted, but it has been fun. I have made hundreds of mistakes, experiencing unlimited forgiveness from God's people. I have also had the incredible privilege to meet thousands of people from all walks of life. I have been able to go places I did not know even existed and done things I did not know could even be done. I have been with people in some of their greatest joys and successes, as well as experienced with them their deepest disappointments and grief. There is nothing like the world of ministry.

Not all of it has been fun. I have been accused, maligned, lied about, and sometimes filled with fear. At times, I have read about this guy in the paper I did not recognize, and yet he had the same name as me. Oh no, it *was* me! I have been very disappointed and at times even depressed. In this world of ministry, I can go from the top of Mount Everest to the bottom of the ocean all within just a matter of minutes. Even if only one of the 25 e-mails I receive in a day is negative, it is the only one I seem to remember the rest of the day. If you have not gotten it yet, there is nothing like the world of ministry.

I have a burning fire in my heart to share some of the things I have learned in ministry. In most of these things, I feel like I am just a beginner in ranks. In fact, the longer I operate in this world, the more I know I do not know and the more I want to learn. There is nothing like learning and living life in the ministry world.

This book is for ministers of all ages, in all seasons of ministry, serving in any ministry role, in any size ministry, located in any part of the world. The top ten things I have learned in my ministry journey serve as the thrust of this book. I am convinced that most, if not all, of these things transcend beyond the ministry world into the world of life, business, and influence.

I have had the unique privilege as a pastor to live and learn life from an extremely varied group of people: farmers, ranchers, private business owners, housewives, educators, entrepreneurs, politicians, lawyers, doctors, technicians, engineers, refinery workers, junior executives, coaches, presidents, fishermen, chief executive officers, economists, chairmen of the boards of corporate America, and many others. This special world of people has taught me so much about myself, life, and ministry. Come with me on this journey. I can guarantee you one thing: There is nothing like it in the world.

1

THE POWER OF
ONE HOUR

FOCUS CAN MAKE A DIFFERENCE in your life. When you focus for a set amount of time, this difference elevates into becoming an impact. When discipline joins focus, you can change your world, and ministers need to be world-changers.

I have always had a passion to change the world. I believe when God calls you, He gives you an insatiable passion to want to make a difference with your life. When you are making a difference, peace abides. When you are not, discontentment abounds.

Discontentment in ministry occurs for many reasons. The seed of discontentment is born when our lens becomes blurred. What we see and how we see things will determine so much about life. It will also determine whether or not you are changing the world.

In this busy, fast-paced, high-tech, schedule-driven world, we can lose our focus very easily. In other words, the lens can become very blurred. This is why we strive to formulate the discipline of focus.

I cannot control various events and decisions made in Northwest Arkansas, any more than I can control them in Washington, D.C., Atlanta, Dallas, Tokyo, London, or Jerusalem. I cannot determine the attitudes of the people in my own church, or better yet, even my own staff team.

> **WHAT WOULD HAPPEN IN YOUR LIFE AND MINISTRY IF YOU FOCUSED FOR ONE HOUR DAILY ON ONE THING ALONE?**

What I can control is my focus. Even when I may not want to or feel like it, I am convinced that I can bridle and train myself to focus.

What would happen in your life and ministry if you focused for one hour daily on one thing alone? What would happen if your focus was so tight for that one hour that it was as piercing as a laser beam? I believe you would begin to discover the power of one hour.

LET ME TELL YOU A STORY

When I was in college, I received one of the greatest challenges in life and ministry I have ever received. It was not in a classroom for theology or ministry, even though I was challenged there. The challenge did not pertain to my dating life or my financial status. The challenge came from a man of God.

I traveled with a friend to the Dallas and Fort Worth metroplex to attend a Bible conference. My friend's dad was on the speaking circuit for conferences such as these. He called his son and told him that he could get us in the presence of a man of God if we desired. We were hungry and thirsty for God, so the decision was easy.

Following the late dismissal of that worship session, a man of God who had preached that evening denied himself and went to dinner with a couple of young preachers. As we ate dinner that night, he mentored us. He answered many questions and just loved us with biblical and practical truth.

Just before we left, I asked him this question: *"If you could tell me one thing I could do as a minister that would really make a difference, what would it be?"* I really thought he would tell me about some ministry or repeat to me some sermon he had preached. He did not.

Without any hesitancy, he made a statement I have never forgotten to this day. He looked at me from under his bushy eyebrows with piercing eyes and said: *"Ronnie, if you could begin to spend one hour a day with God, there is no telling what God will do with you."* He did not call it what I call it, but he introduced me on that late night to the principle of "the power of one hour."

I was young and dumb, but hungry and thirsty for God. I did not have any better sense than to implement that principle immediately. I am so glad the Holy Spirit enabled me to do so. I have learned the power of one hour.

A DEFINING MOMENT

What the Lord gave me that night was a defining moment. That moment has impacted and made a difference in my life as much as anything in these years of ministry.

It became a defining moment for me personally even to this day, for my family in every way, for every church I have served, especially the people of God I have shepherded for these 20 years consecutively, and for the ministry God has given me across the world. Without that moment, I probably would have become shipwrecked because of the challenges of the ministry. I promise you that I would have become very disillusioned with life and ministry. My ego and drive would have been like a car out of control on an icy road. The lens through which I viewed everything would have become very blurry.

Through the years, this hour with God has taken on all kinds of appearances and levels of maturity. Even though it occurred in various ways while in college and during my early seminary days, it was while working on my master's and doctoral degrees that it became stamped on my heart to take place in the early morning. Even though my full-time pastorate was one hour from the seminary I was attending four days a week, I was faithful to observe the power of one hour.

This defining moment not only defined me, but also defined my ministry calling and church. You can give your life to a thousand issues daily. You must give yourself to God daily.

As a minister, I am not talking about sermon preparation time. I am talking about letting God speak to your life through His Word. I am talking about you becoming the prayer warrior God wills you to become. I am talking about you letting God lead you into some deep moments with Him that will impact everything you do. You know, change your world.

I have discovered through the years that the degree to which God changes me will usually be the degree to which I change the world. I cannot expect to change "the world" until I let God have more than ample opportunity to "change my world by changing me first."

Five days a week, my day begins far before dawn as love for God, His Word, my needs, ministry, and discipline call me to my initial hour with God. If travel occurs, it usually interrupts the early morning to a degree. On Friday and Saturday, I try to sleep in later, just to ensure my body is prepared for my Super Bowl each Sunday which is the Lord's Day. Regardless of the day or the location or the challenge, I do not compromise the power of that hour I spend with God.

THE STEAM ENGINE

Rest assured, it is not legalism to me. I am a man in which grace abounds. This is not about me feeling like I am spiritual, and doesn't serve as one more thing I must check off of my daily task list. No, this is about God showing me many years ago that my walk with Him would be like the steam engine of an old locomotive train.

Would you use your imagination for a moment? Imagine a locomotive train of years ago. You had the steam engine, the cars, and the caboose. Life and ministry is filled with many of the cars on that train. The final car, the caboose of life, is usually as they say, "the tail that wags the dog." Somehow it disengages from the other cars, or if you are not careful, becomes more significant than the steam engine itself.

By design and verified in history, where the steam engine went, the cars followed, even the caboose. The power of the steam engine was tied to one thing: the power of the wood or coal that was shoveled in to keep the engine burning effectively.

Your personal walk with God becomes your steam engine in the train of life and ministry. When disarray and disorder are occurring, your walk can keep you aligned enough to keep the cars on the track of life, heading in the right direction. Sometimes you sense they are off the track and they are, but how you view what is happening will be determined by one thing: your perspective. You know, the way you see things.

Your personal walk with God that receives focus on the first hour of the day, every day, will help you keep the lens clear. What will it take? Focus and discipline.

REALITIES

Reality television is huge in media markets today. It just cuts through the stuff and gives you the actual reality that is happening. People are sick and tired of plastic ministers building plastic churches. This is why authenticity is now the buzz. Get real with me.

Reality #1

Your walk with God determines everything about your life. This does not mean that life will not have moments of suffering or challenge. Suffering will always be a part of life. What it does mean is that the degree to which you walk with God will determine the degree of everything else you experience in life.

Through your walk with God, you will keep perspective. Through your walk, you will eventually know where the Lord is leading you. Through your walk, you will have the power to endure the challenges of church life today. Through your walk, you will gain insight and wisdom for decision-making. Through your walk, you can live above the temptations and ethical challenges of our culture. Through your walk, you will be able to win over the flaming missiles that are hurled toward you by Satan himself.

> SATAN IS OUT TO DESTROY MINISTERS AND CHURCHES. IT IS OUR WALK WITH GOD THAT CAN BE THE ARTILLERY TO WIN OVER HIS DEMONIC FORCES.

Satan is out to destroy ministers and churches. It is our walk with God that can be the artillery to win over his demonic forces. As your walk with God goes, so goes the rest of your life.

Reality #2

As you deepen your walk with God, He will broaden your influence. This does not mean you will be the next Billy Graham, Rick Warren, T.D. Jakes, or Joel Osteen. God alone determines whom He raises up, not us. We cannot manipulate Him in any way.

What we can do is deepen our walk with Him. Usually when this occurs, there is something that happens with our influence. God seems to open doors in our relationships, opportunities, and ministry. He seems to be able to trust us with more because He knows He is our life, and our walk with Him is superior to all other people, places, or things.

You cannot expect God to do the miraculous if you are not focused on your personal walk with Him. You cannot expect God to do something *through* you if you are not allowing Him to work *in* you every day of your life.

God expanding your influence does not guarantee a bigger ministry or church. You have missed it if you equate the two. It means that wherever you are serving you are not only being faithful, but fruitful. You are being fruitful *beyond* the level of your giftedness, *beyond* your church's resources, and living in the supernatural lane of ministry. If you want to see what God will do through you, it all begins with what God is doing in you.

> GOD EXPANDING YOUR INFLUENCE DOES NOT GUARANTEE A BIGGER MINISTRY OR CHURCH. YOU HAVE MISSED IT IF YOU EQUATE THE TWO. IT MEANS THAT WHEREVER YOU ARE SERVING YOU ARE NOT ONLY BEING FAITHFUL, BUT FRUITFUL.

Ministers forfeit their leadership, influence, and ministry when they do not spend time with God daily. Honestly, you even forfeit your paycheck. If your love for God and His Word does not exude enough through you that you desire to make a difference, then reality should tell you that this needs to change in your life.

You cannot control the world, or even various facets of your world. What you can do is focus in on one hour every day that will give you the potential to see things the way God does as He empowers you to live and minister supernaturally.

Reality #3

The power of one hour transcends into every segment of life. Even though I have concentrated on the power of one hour with God and what it will do in your life and ministry, do not forget this principle crosses over into every segment of life. *Do not settle!* You can become more in your life.

If you give yourself to doing anything for one hour a day consistently, you have the potential to become an expert. You have the potential to become proficient in something that you may know little about today.

Just think how great you would feel physically if you gave yourself five days a week to one hour of exercise. The reality is that 30 minutes a day, five days a week consistently with the proper diet can send you into a new orbit physically. The result will not only be that you will feel and look better, but it will also have impact in every area of your life. This is why focus and discipline are both essential.

Imagine what you could learn if for one hour a day you e-mailed, called, and surfed the web, just to learn about great churches and what they are doing to set them apart. Wherever you are serving, that ministry can be impacted by the knowledge you gain from other churches. Of course, you do have to filter it through your own culture and personal giftedness, but your church *will* become more effective.

What do you want to know more about? What do you want to become better at doing? Apply "the power of one hour" principle with focus and discipline and you will be amazed at what occurs.

While learning and living this lesson, I believe you will change your world. The power of one hour with God that occurs with focus and discipline consistently will create a ministry world full of adventure and spiritual power. Remember, there is nothing like it in the world.

> **Remember:** *"So, couldn't you stay awake with Me one hour? Stay awake and pray, so that you won't enter into temptation. The spirit is willing, but the flesh is weak"* (Matt. 26:40–41).

2

WHO YOU ARE
IS MORE IMPORTANT
THAN WHAT YOU DO

MINISTRY IS AN ADVENTURE. Even the most passive minister deals with risks and unforeseeable danger. At the same time, all ministers have the capacity to experience a remarkable, God-sized ministry. Whichever extreme you may see yourself in, or a combination of the two, you are on an adventure. This adventure is unlike anything else in the world.

Ministry continues to change dramatically. When I entered this adventure, it was easy compared to the challenges we face today. There have always been certain churches that operate like war zones. When you minister in a church in our generation, you are entering dangerous territory, not seasonally, but daily.

This is why it is important to know who you are. As the challenges escalate in number and intensify in debate, you must understand who you are.

CHALLENGES

The common layperson in your church has no idea of these challenges. No one understands these better than your colleagues in ministry. The size or location of your church does not exempt you from any of these contemporary challenges. Let me identify just a few of these unique challenges.

Carnal Christians

You would think the church of Corinth has become the model for the church today. Division, conflict, immorality, confusing theology, and majoring on the minors all serve as indicators of the correlation between the Corinthian church and the church of the 21st century. Taking the good news of Jesus to the world, personal holiness, and love seem to be forgotten commodities in most churches.

Yes, I believe we are experiencing some of the greatest outpourings of God upon some churches. However, at the same time, those churches are rare in our culture. Even those few

> **TAKING THE GOOD NEWS OF JESUS TO THE WORLD, PERSONAL HOLINESS, AND LOVE SEEM TO BE FORGOTTEN COMMODITIES IN MOST CHURCHES.**

churches deal with the carnality of Christians just like you do.

I am amazed at the thousands of churches that dismiss their ministers or have their ministers leave under fire. The size and visibility of the church does not guarantee protection from this injustice. It is happening in churches of all sizes, located in all places, and is going on with ministers everywhere. This is why you need to know who you are.

Dysfunctional Churches

Over time, carnal Christians create very dysfunctional churches. When ministers stoop into carnality, they may lead their church to become spiritually dysfunctional, creating chaos. If a church does not determine its daily practice and operation by the Bible, believing it to be the only source of authority, the church will become dysfunctional. When the church disconnects from biblical authority in belief and daily practice, chaos will occur.

Minister failure has contributed to creating these dysfunctional, carnal churches. Ministers fail morally when they cease to experience personal devotion before the Lord daily. When a minister goes through moral or ethical failure, usually the church is negatively influenced for decades.

The greatest protection you have from contributing to this unspiritual, carnal dysfunction, and to lead through it if you have inherited a church with it, is to know who you are.

High Expectations

Unreasonable expectations from God's people have placed ministers under a very unfair scrutiny. There have always been those who were not reasonable in their expectations of ministers, but today it is different. This escalating explosion has increased the danger zone for all of us. This is why you must know who you are.

As we navigate through the waters of high expectations, we do not need to contribute to it. We need to promise to do only what we can do and will do. Our motto needs to be: *"Under-promise, over-deliver."* Do not promise to do things you will not do, but strive to over-deliver what you have promised you would do or you know you should do.

Flavors of Church

Walking into the church today is far different than the "one size fits all" culture of years gone by. When you minister in a church in this contemporary world, it is like walking into Baskin-Robbins trying to determine the kind of ice cream you desire. Men and the way they built their church in their culture have now taken over the nomenclature. This results in shallow questions from shallow Christians.

The common question among ministers today is, "What is your model?" From that point, they move into naming men and their categorical models. The Word of God and Jesus' model seldom enter into the discussion. Why is this happening?

> MOST CHRISTIANS AND MANY CHURCHES HAVE THEOLOGY THAT LOOKS LIKE THE FINISHED PRODUCT OF COLD STONE CREAMERY. IT IS COMPOSED OF A LITTLE BIT OF THIS AND A LITTLE BIT OF THAT, RESULTING IN THEIR PERSONAL THEOLOGICAL WONDER THAT WOULD NEVER MAKE IT IF FILTERED THROUGH THE WORD OF GOD

One of the great places I enjoy going when I am in Texas or Florida is Cold Stone Creamery. This ice cream phenomenon involves not only the basic flavor you desire, but also picking and choosing added substances or one of their customized wonders. It is a marvelous place to go.

Most Christians and many churches have theology that looks like the finished product of Cold Stone Creamery. It is composed of a little bit of this and a little bit of that, resulting in their personal theological wonder that would never make it if filtered through the Word of God. This is why you need to know who you are.

Technological Phenomenon

Technology has changed not only the world, but even the church. E-mail convenience, message boards, and websites have become disasters to ministers. Battle formulation and the attack strategy have been mobilized toward ministers, churches, and even denominations.

I believe technology has been given to us by God himself for the purpose of taking the good news of Jesus to the entire world. Technology does not exist to create church division, impair the reputation of ministers, formulate battle strategy, or cripple denominations, any more than technology was created to promote pornography. This is why you really need to know who you are. These are new discoveries for a carnal church. Our goal should always be to use the gift of technology to advance the gospel globally and build up fellow believers regionally and locally.

Human Tradition

In my 30 years of leading local churches, I have seen laypersons fight more for their human traditions than for biblical truth. This has resulted in needless debate, breeding a culture of what I call "spiritual humanism." Spiritual humanism occurs when we attempt to spiritualize "our way of doing things," rather than doing what God says we should do according to the Bible, ensuring that the will of God is done in the church.

As a minister of the gospel, this can create turbulent air in any church, especially one that is led by a minister or a team of ministers who want to do things God's way. You have to be personal, relational, understanding, wise, and genuine to deal with this detractor to growth.

Use wisdom concerning the issues and the timing of dealing with them or else you may become a victim of the guard. This serves as another reason to know who you are.

One of the great attributes of our church in Northwest Arkansas since the 1970s is that we have been a church committed to doing things God's way. I am truly the under-shepherd, serving the ultimate Shepherd of our church, Jesus Christ. It is an amazing story and a wonderful testimony that a church can be built upon and by God's Word anywhere.

WHO YOU ARE IS MORE IMPORTANT THAN WHAT YOU DO

This is a great principle that every minister must know. When you serve in this unique world called church, you will face each challenge listed above and even many more. As you face these challenges, the pressure is unimaginable. You face the pressure internally. Each of us loves to be liked by all people. This is an unrealistic expectation. Your goal should be to never let anyone outside of your circle of love, regardless of their treatment toward you; but the pressure you face internally demands that you know who you are or else you will make one of the most tragic errors in ministry life. You will become more concerned about what you do than who you are. This creates a spiritual disorder within you that chokes the life of God and ministry out of you.

You also face the pressure externally. Heaped upon your own personal challenge is the pressure of others trying to conform you into their mold or desires. Your network, your association of churches, your conference peers, your human tradition, your church, or your denomination may serve as added pressure you will face from others. Their desires for you (which are many times filled with good intentions) or their unrealistic expectations of you can get you into doing things you do not want to do, do not have a passion to do, are not gifted to do, do not have time to do, or that God just does not want you to do. This will result in you feeling very unfulfilled, frustrated, and filled with anxiety you do not need. This has occurred and will continue to repeat itself when you forget that who you are is more important than what you do.

Regardless of the internal and external pressures upon you, please remember: *Who you are is more important than what you do.* How can you process this, applying it both personally and in ministry? I believe you do so in these ways.

Biblically

I believe every minister and church needs to go deep into the first chapter of the Book of Ephesians. We need to learn for the first time, or refresh our memories on what God says about each one of us. I discovered this again and taught this to our people recently for five weeks under the theme: *"Who Am I?"* People were freed. The personal heritage, personal insecurities, and the abusive ways, words, and expectations of others place most Christians in the prison cells of bondage. Therefore, people begin to "gain their identity" more from "what they do," than from "who they are." This is not God's will.

You are a minister. Go into the Bible text found in Ephesians 1:3–14, take it apart, maintain balance, and learn who you are in Christ. It will change everything about you. On the last day of the series, I gave out a printed statement the size of a postcard for people to remember what I had taught them for those five weeks. These words have gone all over the world. The statement on the postcard reads:

WHO AM I?
In Jesus Christ,
I am chosen miraculously, accepted completely,
forgiven freely, planned providentially,
and rich spiritually.

I read through that statement almost daily. I keep it in my prayer journal to remind me of who I am in Jesus Christ.

Functionally

Once you realize what God says about who you are as a Christian, you are ready to deal functionally with your calling as a minister. Church and minister dysfunction happen because of biblical and functional misunderstanding.

For every pastor, you are the God-called leader of your church. You are to be the spiritual thermostat and leader of that body. You serve by God's calling, but you are also there to serve God's people. As a pastor, I believe you are called to be a feeder, leader, and interceder. These are your three priorities functionally as you lead your church to fulfill the Great Commission of Jesus Christ.

As the pastor, the ministry of teaching and preaching is vital for you to fulfill the function of your calling. Feeding God's people from the Word of God is the first of your ministry assignments. Leading God's people toward God's will and goal is essential in your function as the pastor. God does not call you to conform to your people, drive your people, lord over your people, or abuse your people; but He calls you to lead them as a shepherd does his sheep. Interceding for God's people is also very important in your function as a pastor. The ministry of prayer is imperative on the agenda of a God-called pastor.

> I BELIEVE YOU ARE CALLED TO BE A FEEDER, LEADER, AND INTERCEDER. THESE ARE YOUR THREE PRIORITIES FUNCTIONALLY AS YOU LEAD YOUR CHURCH TO FULFILL THE GREAT COMMISSION OF JESUS CHRIST.

As a minister on the staff of a local church, you serve at the will of your pastor. You are there to lift his arms up so he can fulfill the above three functional aspects of his calling. You are there to partner with him to see your church fulfill the Great Commission of Jesus Christ. You are there to help him fulfill his calling as pastor-teacher of the church. If you imagine yourself to be anything other than one who fulfills these functions in your church, you are deceived. If you disagree with him, do so in private. If people come to you about him, defend him. If you cannot resolve your differences with him, leave quietly. However, if he commits immorality or heresy, confront and expose him.

As a minister that may be part of a para-church ministry or employed by a denomination, your role is to come alongside the pastor as well as the church for the sole purpose of assisting them in some way to fulfill the Great Commission of Jesus Christ. You serve that church as an extension of that pastor, assisting him with your calling, gifts, and resources. This will result in great fellowship and the kingdom of God being advanced.

Personally

Once we understand what the Bible says about our identity in Jesus Christ and who we are in Him, and once we carry out that identity in our various functional roles in ministry, we need to remember one more key ingredient so we will not get caught in the trap of believing that what we do is more important than who we are. We can escape that trap and live God's way when we remember these things personally.

Ministry is a supernatural calling. You are doing ministry out of calling, not preference. Your calling from God is the only thing that will keep you in it. From time to time, revisit your ministry calling. Revisit it from the day you were first called by God, and then revisit the time when God called you to where you are presently serving. The minister who forgets his calling will become ensnared in the trap of performance.

God has bestowed upon you spiritual gifts. Ensure those gifts are being exercised where you are serving. If not, the trap will bite you. You will begin to identify your worth with your performance or on what you do, forgetting who you are in Jesus Christ and what He has gifted you to do.

Carnal chaos does not have to take place. When it does, it creates a ministry world that is not reflective of God's Word and does not bring glory to Jesus Christ. Know biblically, functionally, and personally who you are. Ministers have to learn and be reminded daily: *Who you are is more important than what you do.*

When you live this principle, there is nothing like it in the world.

Remember: *"For in Him the entire fullness of God's nature dwells bodily, and you have been filled by Him, who is the head over every ruler and authority"* (Col. 2:9–10).

3

PRACTICE
DETERMINES PLAY

"THE AMERICAN CHURCH IN CRISIS" is the glaring title of an article in *Outreach Magazine* in the May/June 2006 edition. This echoes its cover, which speaks of research showing that declining attendance is taking place in the churches of America. I can capture the heartbeat of the issue when it reports:

> Numbers from actual counts of people in Orthodox Christian churches (Catholic, mainline, and evangelical) show that in 2004, **17.7% of the population attended a Christian church on any given weekend.**

This data came from tracking two-thirds of the 330,000 orthodox Christian churches and using a formula to guesstimate the remaining one-third of churches.

By watching the various denominations and their annual reports, they were becoming convinced of this decline before their actual research was completed. Unequivocally, the American church is in crisis. This comes as no shock to me.

With all the resources available to the church, we are showing little for it. What is the problem? The decline is real in most churches and in many, the trend seems irreversible. The attendance declination represents the declination in the spiritual health of these churches. Yes, I am confident that some are declining due to the village, town, or region in which they are located, because sometimes a transition happens in communities which can be very difficult and devastating to a church and its work. With that caveat, I want to speak to what I believe the real issue may be.

Some problems are symptomatic, and I believe the declination of church attendance is a symptom. Looking deeper, the real issue is the spiritual health of the church. You must look to the very deepest level, the root, to find the real issue.

> SOME PROBLEMS ARE SYMPTOMATIC, AND I BELIEVE THE DECLINATION OF CHURCH ATTENDANCE IS A SYMPTOM. LOOKING DEEPER, THE REAL ISSUE IS THE SPIRITUAL HEALTH OF THE CHURCH.

The real issue is the minister. Remember, I am one of you, just like you in many ways. I deal with your challenges, problems, and opportunities. However, it is time for excuse-making to be eliminated from our vocabulary. The "if this" or "but you do not understand" and "if only we had" all need to be checked at the door. They are excuses, nothing more.

At the root of the church being in crisis are the minister and his life. This is really astounding when you consider how ministers may have more education than ever before. Beyond basic academic preparation, continuing education is available to all of us. There are more conferences to attend than you could attend in 100 lifetimes. There are more opportunities via the Internet than one has time to even investigate, much less use.

Ministers are somewhat like many great athletes who squander their opportunity for success. These athletes have all of the tools, but they forfeit their opportunity many times due to poor decision-making that leads them to loss. They love the Friday night lights or the loud stadiums on Saturday or the money because they get to play on Sunday. Yet poor decision-making forfeits these benefits and so much more.

As ministers, we have access to something far more powerful than athletic ability. We have the power of God. We have influence which far outlasts the thrill of a crowd or stadium. We even have the investment we make guaranteed in eternity. For some reason, it is just not clicking with us. Why?

Our daily practice habits are questionable and inconsistent. You are no different than a great athlete. *The way you practice daily will determine the way you play.* You get what you get ready for in life. Due to poor decision-making, your practice may be lacking. Therefore, do not be surprised at where your church may be spiritually, numerically, or strategically. *How you practice daily will determine the way you play.* In other words, practice determines play.

What you do daily will result in some kind of product. The product may be good or the product may be mediocre to bad. Would you investigate honestly the way you practice? Life is not a dress rehearsal. Ministry is not a profession. It is incumbent on you to honestly evaluate the way you practice.

PRIORITIES

Decision-making occurs as a result of priorities. Practicing poor priorities will result in play that is not friendly to church health and growth. Personal imbalance will create ministry vertigo. Life lived like a whirlwind will result in ministry dizziness. Somehow, the minister has to rise above whirlwind living. I believe that not only having the right priorities but also practicing them is the secret. What are the right priorities? How should these rank in life?

Personal Relationship and Fellowship with God

Our personal relationship and fellowship with God is more important than anything else. Its priority in your life ranks above the latest church crisis or unrealistic church expectation. Nothing, and I mean nothing, should rise above this priority. If it does, the result will be an unhealthy life, family, and church. You are good, but you are not good enough to live life, lead a family, and shepherd a church without a daily practice time with the Father above. The way you practice this spiritual discipline will result in the way you live, learn, teach, pastor, and lead.

Family

Your family is more important than your church family. I am convinced that many minister's families are in crisis because the leader of the family is out taking care of every one else other than his own family. He is out praying at some function rather than praying with his family. He is away at some meeting rather than living up to some agreed-upon meeting with his family. I will speak to this priority in detail in the next chapter.

Church as a Ministry

There are seasons in every profession, and ministry is not an exception to this rule. People will die on your day off. Funerals will occur whether you are on vacation or not. Particular times in a minister's ministry will be very busy due to a needed emphasis like a festival, pageant, campaign, or revival meeting. Keep it in perspective. Keep people at the heartbeat of all you do.

Church as a Job

So many things we do "in the name of church" may not be as important as we deem them to be. For example, you may decide to "stop by the office" when there is really no need. You may decide to check your e-mail one more time before you retire for the evening, rather than go into your child's room and tuck him or her into bed. If you have not yet figured this out about ministry, remember this: *there will always be something to do*. Keep the *job* part of your church life in perspective. Working in ministry is great and I love it. At the same time, we cannot let our love for it be used as an excuse to not do real ministry with people, or more importantly be with our family, or even more importantly than all of that, relate and fellowship with God daily.

Recreation

Ministers are no different than other people. We can fall as prey before the god of recreation and play. Nothing is killing the family any more today than people living improper and imbalanced lives because they believe their kids will be the next Michael Jordan, Joe Montana, Mia Hamm, or Carrie Underwood. Spiritual wisdom has been kicked out the door of Christian families' homes as they follow their kids through life. Minister,

> THE WAY YOU PREPARE WILL DETERMINE THE WAY YOU PLAY.

get a grip! Get perspective and give your people some perspective. I love play. I love recreation. I love sports. However, it is far down on my priority list. It will never make it above the priorities mentioned above. Balance will only occur when spiritual wisdom is followed.

A minister has the challenge of practicing the right priorities. The way you live life and do ministry will reflect your personal priorities.

PREPARATION

The way you prepare will determine the way you play. I wish this worked differently, but it does not. It dawned on me about two years ago when I was really evaluating my life, time, and schedule. Most of my life is given toward preparation. It seems I am always preparing for something. My time in preparation far exceeds my time in actual execution. I want to give you a window into my life.

Personal

The early morning has become a time when I commit myself to the art of preparation. On Sundays through Thursdays, I arise between 3:30 and 4:00 a.m. to begin my day with God. In that first hour, I give myself to God in personal devotion. I follow a plan to pray that God gives me along the way. Usually, this involves some type of prayer list or agenda.

However, your prayer time must be controlled by the Holy Spirit. In this first hour, I also have practiced reading through the Bible annually. I have done this since 1990, and I have found it very enriching and insightful. It is surprising to me how many ministers have never read the Bible all the way through, yet we are to be the spiritual leaders of the church.

After that first hour or so, I give myself to sermon preparation. Above all, the minister has to be prepared for his calling. The early morning is critical to this preparation time. I usually study a minimum of three to five hours each morning. In the time I spend at my home office for this preparation, usually 40–60 minutes is spent in exercise and eating breakfast. On a typical day, I will walk 40 minutes, enjoying that most days as time to dialogue with my wife. Additionally, one hour or so is given in the mornings to correspondence via e-mail or preparing for meetings of the day or making phone calls to prepare for upcoming matters. There is always something to prepare for in life.

Schedule

I have just informed you of my early to mid-morning schedule, but let me continue on, because preparation continues. Usually by 10:15 a.m. or so, I am preparing to present myself to the public. By 11:20 a.m. or so, I am driving toward a lunch appointment. On Monday through Thursday, I never waste a lunch time. This is always one hour or so, a time when I can just hang out with people or accomplish a task with a person or group. I make myself available to all of my lay people for lunch times, as well as all of my staff team.

By 1:00 to 1:15 p.m., unless it was a working luncheon, I am in the office. I spend my time answering e-mail, returning phone calls, or doing some kind of correspondence. Additionally, the afternoon is given to meetings I have prepared to lead or meetings in which I just need to be informed of various matters or my input is needed. It is my goal that by 5:30 or 6:00 p.m. I am in my car traveling home to be with my family or having a time of fellowship or possibly even conducting some kind of needed meeting.

I give myself to this schedule wholeheartedly on Sunday through Thursday so that I can do little to nothing on Friday, except what Jeana and I want to do together. I will speak about my Fridays in the next chapter.

On Saturdays, I sleep in until 7:30 a.m. or so, having my time with God for the first hour, and then I enter into a time of mastering the message for Sunday, trying to commit as much of it as possible to memory. Usually, after this additional 60–120 minutes, I try to do as little as possible or just do what I want to do. It is rare that Jeana and I do anything away from home on Saturday nights. Even though I may not go to sleep until after 10:00 p.m. or so, I am lying in bed just resting or reading or watching something on television by 8:30 p.m.

You can see from what I have shared about my schedule that my life is given to huge amounts of preparation. The actual execution of a sermon message or an actual meeting or appointment is minimal compared to the preparation it took.

Passion

I believe when God calls a person to serve Him in ministry, He injects that person with passion. Let's take Pastor Allen for a moment. He doesn't have to have someone "pump him up" daily. From his walk with Christ personally to his work ethic daily and to his service to the Lord on Sundays, he is contagious and infectious with his passion. People buy into Allen's vision for their church.

When ministry and life begin to squeeze a minister, we find out what that minister is made of in life and ministry. In contrast to Pastor Allen, let's take Pastor Larry. He is slow to rise daily, finally getting to the office after a number of things he finds himself doing. He lives and leads all over the map. His secretary or colleagues never really know where he is because he can be anywhere from helping his wife at home in the day with the children (not answering his cell phone, pretending he is involved in ministry), to practicing his golf game with the Green family, or just driving without any direction at all. He fills his time with whatever hits him at the time. Why? He is passionless. Sad to say, but there are more Pastor Larrys in ministry than Pastor Allens!

If you play the way you practice your priorities and preparation, you will play by the passion in which you have practiced daily. How passionate of a person are you? Are you enthusiastic about your faith and about your calling?

Passion is non-negotiable in shepherding and leadership. You have to believe in what you are doing. You have to enjoy what you are doing. Passion is caught from you, not taught!

Passionate leaders get people to believe again. Passionate leaders are able to rally people to a better future. Passionate leaders are able to communicate with heart opportunities that are present. Passionate leaders can infect an organization with vision. Ministers must be passionate leaders. Without passion, you will lead no one anywhere.

Ministers are seen at times as being cautious and reserved. Ministers are also seen as low risk-takers and as being caretakers. This is why churches and ministries are declining. Churches

> **PASSION IS NON-NEGOTIABLE IN SHEPHERDING AND LEADERSHIP. YOU HAVE TO BELIEVE IN WHAT YOU ARE DOING.**

decline when passion is missing. When people come to your church, they need to see passion — passion from the parking lot to the pew to the pulpit! Passion is enthusiasm. If you are not enthusiastic about Jesus and His church and ministry, why should they be?

Passionate people are powerful. Passionate people are assertive. Passionate people are sincere. Passionate people are secure. Passionate people are infectious. Passionate people see opportunity. Passionate people are believers in "the now."

Pray for passion. Practice passion. Live with passion. Lead with passion.

WORLD-CLASS EXCELLENCE

A world-class leader is committed to excellence. A world-class leader is committed to the details. A world-class leader puts it on the stage in the highest manner whether he is leading one person or ten thousand people. When something is world class, it is done with excellence. Are you committed to excellence? Are you practicing excellence?

Excellence on Sunday will not happen when you are sleeping in on Monday. The relentless return of the Sabbath will get you! Excellence is doing something in the highest manner with the resources you have available. Excellence is not determined by the size of your church membership or your town, but by your commitment to it. It begins with an attitude. It comes when a standard is set. Excellence may cost a little more in the short term, but mediocrity always costs more in the long term.

Church facilities and grounds show your commitment to excellence. The way you welcome people needs to be done with excellence, from the parking lot to the door to the center in which worship is experienced. Our motto should be, *"Excellence in all things and all things to the glory of God!"*

Horstz Schultze branded the excellent service given by the world-class Ritz Carlton Hotels and Resorts. By his testimony, they were so committed to excellence that after they noticed on which side of the bed you slept, that would be the side of the bed you found your slippers when you arrived back at your room from your activities of the day. He has now left the Ritz Carlton in order to establish a hotel brand that exceeds even this state-of-the-art pacesetting organization.

If a hotel can have that kind of world-class excellence, the minister and the church should do even more for our God. Lazy preparation, sloppy attention to details, and mediocrity have cost many churches influence in the lives of people. Details win championships for teams. Details attended to during the week will result in details being tended to on Sundays. World-class excellence is the commitment of ministers who want to give their best to God and to their people.

LEARNING

We need to practice learning every day. The way you learn and what you learn will determine the way you play. You will reproduce before others what you are and what you have learned. Are you a chronic learner?

Arrogance says you know it all. Arrogance believes others can teach you little. Arrogance is deceiving. Arrogance has cost many ministers a relationship with their families and churches.

Living is about learning. I heard this statement many years ago: *You will never be any greater than the places you go, the people you meet, or the books you read.* I believe it! Have you been anywhere *new* lately, or are you still going to the same old boring places? Have you hung out with any one *new* in your life lately? Have you read a book, perhaps even a book that is not Christian-based or helping you in ministry? Expand yourself and you will expand your leadership. Learn while you live.

When you learn while you live, you will learn as you lead. You will always be aware that someone may have a better idea than you. You will become aware that many people have greater insight on issues than you. You will learn from your experiences, including your failures. You may even learn to laugh at yourself! I did not do this very well early on, but the older I get, the more I laugh at myself. Minister, do yourself a favor and laugh at yourself, even in some of your leadership miscues that are not deadly. In other words, just learn from your own leadership and from the leadership of others. There are many gifted people out there in your church and, believe it or not, some are more gifted than you.

ADJUSTING

Speaking of learning, one of the great lessons of life is to learn to adjust. Regardless of what you have planned, adjustment may be necessary for your own sake, your family, or even your church. We have to learn to align our lives by the will of God. This alignment requires adjustment.

Adjustment is change. Change is my friend and my fuel! I do not perceive change as my enemy, but as my friend. Change does not drain me, but fuels me. How do you deal with change?

Churches cannot be paralyzed in the 20th century if churches are going to be successful in the 21st century. Change is essential.

This is why we must practice change. Change will determine how we play in the culture. If we want the world to see us as relevant, then change is necessary.

I was talking the other night with a group of young pastors, all of whom had come through my own ministry. I was conversing with them about the status of the denomination of which we are a part. One of the great young men said, "Pastor, is it even relevant?" That is a great question for every denomination, church, and minister to ask. We must be relevant.

Relevance is usually determined by the way we respond to change. Our response needs to be timely and wise, always guided by truth. Change for change's sake is stupid! Change with purpose is wise. It is right. It is necessary. We must be a people that not only understand our times, but *adjust to our times*. The message of Jesus' good news is always relevant. The way we package the message in this Christ-less culture has to be adjusted continually.

LET'S PLAY BALL!

A minister has to play ball! He cannot live his ministry in the bullpen or in his study. Sooner or later, he has to step up and play ball! You have to put it on the stage. What you do, how you do it, and the level of success you have when you do it, usually represents the way you practiced and what you have practiced.

Therefore, practice the right priorities daily and order will accompany a balanced life. Practice preparation at the highest level of sacrifice and success will follow. Practice with passion and you will play with passion. Practice by tending to details in the right way, and you will experience world-class excellence in every way. Practice learning and you will live and lead with a teachable spirit. Practice change personally, and you will lead your church to believe that change is their friend and their fuel as they confront their culture with the unalterable, unchangeable, truth of Jesus' good news.

Just maybe the way we practice and what we practice daily as ministers will rescue the church from crisis. I believe it will. We are the key! It is time . . . time to play ball!

Remember: *". . . train yourself in godliness, for the training of the body has a limited benefit, but godliness is beneficial in every way, since it holds promise for the present life and also for the life to come"* (1 Tim. 4:7–8).

4

BUILDING FAMILY IS MORE IMPORTANT THAN BUILDING MINISTRY

I WAS A VERY YOUNG PASTOR in a growing church. I had my academic degrees behind me and was engaged in my pastoral venture — hook, line, and sinker! I was in my late twenties and had been married for just under ten years. Josh was four or five years old and Nick was only one or two years old. I was zooming and filled with life, vitality, and vision.

God was doing some marvelous things in our church. We had seen it come alive with great passion and fire for evangelism. Everything was growing.

I am confident that in my youthful zeal I made several mistakes. I was probably too confident for some to appreciate, and the growth of the church had become a threat to a few others. I understood spiritual warfare to some degree at this time in my life. I had already pastored some churches and was well aware of many of the challenges in this dimension of leadership. However, it emerged to an entirely different and unprecedented level in my life and ministry in this particular church.

It was interesting to watch. We would have heaven on Sunday as God would move profoundly. Attendance was surging, people were being won to Christ, and people were growing in their faith. Yet there were always conflicts and challenges beyond what I had ever encountered at that time in ministry life. Because of my immaturity in life and ministry, I did not handle it all very well, but I was mature enough spiritually to have an ear for God every morning and my heart was to do His will above all things. I discovered that God had me in that church not just for them at that season of their journey, but for me. He wanted to use them to refine me, break me, and bring me to an end of myself. It took me a while to get to this place, but I did get there.

Heaven was happening on Sunday and then trouble returned on Monday. Meetings were dominant in the church world back then, and they seemed to occur nightly and continuously for pastors in that season of American church life. It is important for you to know that Jeana had been raised in a pastor's home, so she understood the challenges of church and family to a degree, but I was exhausted and my family was caught in the middle of it all.

I would hurry home around 5:00 p.m. in order to get back to an early evening meeting with some committee or group of leaders. As stated already, warfare was intense, my family was very young, and the church was growing. I knew it was taking its toll on Jeana and me. The boys were way too young to feel it or know it, but I was neglecting them due to all of the demands on my life.

IN TIME, I BELIEVE
JEANA AND MY FAMILY
BECAME AWARE OF THIS
NEW TRUTH IN MY LIFE,
EVEN TO THE POINT OF
BELIEVING IT. SHE AND
THE BOYS KNEW, "DAD
WILL NOT SACRIFICE
US IN ORDER FOR THE
CHURCH TO GROW."

One night on my journey home, I came to a stop sign. I believe I could take you to it today. It was like the Holy Spirit spoke to me in that still, small convicting voice. I am not sure what occurred, but I am confident of what I told the Lord at that very moment. I said, *"Lord, I will stop sacrificing my family on the altar of ministry success."* That event and moment has shaped my life and family to this very day. God used all of the circumstances to teach me and help me. Had God not taught me that lesson at a young age, it might have been catastrophic later in ministry, marriage, and life.

In time, I believe Jeana and my family became aware of this new truth in my life, even to the point of believing it. She and the boys knew, "Dad will not sacrifice us in order for the church to grow." At the same time, they realized their dad and husband had great responsibilities and his life was not his own, it was God's.

Therefore, I believe that building your family *is* more important than building your ministry. Not only have I believed it, I have lived it. Today it stands as probably the only legacy I will ever see this side of heaven. I would not trade anything for it that ministry offers. My family is a major work of grace and grace alone. God has answered and continues to answer our prayers concerning our family. We have been and are blessed immeasurably.

The people in our church and various pastors regularly ask me, "What did you and Jeana do to get the marriage and family you have?" I can assure you that we did some things wrong, but we also did some things right. We were good learners from our mistakes and from other people we admired, but most of all we learned so much from the Lord and His Word.

As I have evaluated our journey in blending marriage, family, and ministry with balance, I have narrowed the journey to seven values that we observed in our family. These seven values were things we esteemed, believed in, championed, and rewarded continually.

VALUE PRAYER

I realize we are ministers and this sounds like something you would expect another minister to say or try to prove he does, but make no mistake about it: *You will not succeed in marriage, family, and ministry without prayer.* The tango of the three may lead to danger if not done with prayer. Obviously, if you have gotten this far in the book, you have learned of my personal commitment to prayer. With that understood, I will move to how we valued prayer in our family. However, please remember, these suggestions will mean nothing if you do not grow in your own personal prayer life. In fact, this is where most family and ministry battles are won.

Pray the Armor of God on Your Family

For at least two decades I have prayed Ephesians 6:10–18 over my family daily. This passage speaks of the armor of God over the believer. I used to read the passage, but now I pray the specifics of the armor, getting my family ready to face the day. I call their names out to God specifically and then place the armor on them piece by piece. I do this for all of our immediate family.

> THE GREATEST THING YOU CAN DO FOR YOUR FAMILY IS TO HAVE A SPIRITUAL AND ENRICHING MARRIAGE RELATIONSHIP.

We are in a war. Satan goes after your family with great intensity. His will is to destroy your family and church. You cannot give that ground over to him. Therefore, stand your ground in Jesus' name by placing the armor of God on your family in prayer daily.

Pray Specifically Over Your Family

As a minister, be transparent with your family. Prayer makes you transparent. It demonstrates you cannot do it on your own. How can you pray specifically?

Pray with your children before they go to school. We did this daily without exception. Pray through the various crises or situations you face as a family. Pray with your spouse nightly. Jeana and I trade off nightly as to which one of us will pray before we go to sleep.

VALUE MARRIAGE

The greatest thing you can do for your family is to have a spiritual and enriching marriage relationship. If you want your children to make the right decisions in life, especially in relationships, then you have to have a healthy and godly relationship with your spouse. This is a model before them and mentoring in action in the finest fashion.

When you disagree from time to time with your spouse, try not to get into an argument in front of the children. This breeds insecurity and jeopardizes how your child will treat their spouse one day. Mild disagreement may be acceptable, but preserve for your privacy the real verbal struggles. As well, never undermine or demean your mate in front of your children. Get in a room, solve your issues, make up (which can be great!), and move on. The greatest thing you can obtain in marriage and ministry is having a "great forgetter." Leave it alone and press on!

One of the actions I took from the time "the stop sign moment" occurred was that I take off every Friday and spend it with Jeana. It is our day, and I attempt to stay away from the office. I try to delay all church e-mail and phone calls. I tell my people publicly it is my day with Jeana. What do we do on Friday together? Sometimes we hang around the house; we eat lunch together, shop, go to a movie, or enjoy engaging in various activities with our children and now our grandchild. It is rare that I agree to be away speaking somewhere or doing something on Friday. We only do that in either of our schedules if we both agree to it first. This has become one of the greatest days of my week and I look forward to it weekly. When your children and others observe this practice, you personify how valuable your marital relationship really is to you. When you spend uninterrupted time with your mate consistently and weekly, your mate and your children know that your family is more important than your ministry. You can put up with a lot during the week if you know Friday is coming!

VALUE CHURCH

The minister and his family need the church in their lives as much as any other family needs the church. We love the church!

I always told the church when my children were young, "Pray for my children to grow up loving Jesus and the church." Unless something was heavy on my heart, this was always my response anytime I was asked, "How can I pray for your family?" My children love Jesus and the church. Both Josh and Nick married young ladies who love the church.

Josh and Kate, as well as Nick and Meredith, will raise children who love Jesus and the church, beginning with Peyton.

Josh and Nick knew they came before the church, yet they also knew of my great love for the church and responsibility as the pastor of their church. When Josh was experiencing a *once-in-a-lifetime opportunity* to play in the 13-year-old World Series, I did not preach or attend a Sunday night service which I had been scheduled to do. I announced it accordingly on that Sunday morning. This was before it was cool to do such and to miss Sunday night church. Equally, the only game I ever remember missing was when I was asked to preach to Promise Keepers in Washington, D.C., before a million men. I almost chose not to do it, but a friend advised me to talk to my boys and ask them what they thought I should do. Both immediately said, "Go do that!" Parents now are going to the "extreme" and have become very unbalanced in this area. In all they let their children do, they violate church on Sundays. This is dramatically impacting churches, but will also have major negative consequences on their family. I am convinced of it!

Another way to show the value of the church is to tell your children that they receive enormous benefits from being your children. They meet people that most people would never meet and at times experience valuable things that most would never experience. So tell them along the way, "You receive some great benefits because you are a child of a minister, so remember that when you think you may have to give up something because of it."

Concerning church issues, communicate wisely about these with your children. I rarely spoke of any in front of the children and if so, it was only when they were older and we prayed about them as a family.

As a minister, you would do well to have your spouse read this chapter. In fact, have her read it and then talk through it together. Both of you need to understand clearly that your children will catch what you feel, say, and live before them about church. Be careful. Be wise.

VALUE MENTORING WITH GENTLE ACCOUNTABILITY

Teach your children to walk with Christ. Teach your children how to have a daily time with God. Start when they first begin to read words. My boys have had time with God daily since they were very young. They still do today.

Train your children to be leaders. It all starts when they are children. Mentor them to lead and influence others to the degree of their God-given giftedness.

Mentor them in their relationships with friends and then with dating. Do not let them become culture-driven, but encourage them in a godly way to be different if God calls them to be different in something. There were all kinds of relationships where I would at times intervene with my children. I would call a time-out, we would reconsider, and redirect them to other relationships. When Jeana or I did not have peace about something, we would intervene. Why? We knew if Satan captured our children, it would happen through their friends or their dating relationships.

In the early days of having children, I determined I was not running for parenting, but I was already elected. I was accountable to God for my children. Therefore, with gentleness (tamed strength), I would provide accountability. God used both Jeana and I to provide balance in all of those challenges, which were few because the standard was very clear and continually communicated to the boys early on in life.

VALUE CONSISTENCY

Consistency builds godly children. Inconsistency builds the opposite. You must be consistent in your leadership as a parent. You must be consistent in your discipline. Never give up being consistent.

Be honest with your children consistently. Do not play games, trying to get them to guess what you want them to do. You will mess up and make mistakes. When you do, come clean, admit it, and ask their forgiveness. If something happens in your marriage in front of your children, ask them to forgive you.

Be consistent in your schedule with them. Attempt to set a time you will all be together weekly. As our boys got older, this became more difficult, but we made Saturday lunch a time when we would always go out somewhere or stay at home and watch a football game together. As well, we hung out with various families after church on Sunday nights by going out to a light dinner before going home. We made

> YOU WILL MESS UP AND MAKE MISTAKES. WHEN YOU DO, COME CLEAN, ADMIT IT, AND ASK THEIR FORGIVENESS.

Sunday night church an experience by doing this. My point is, be consistent in what you do and what you say.

VALUE COMMUNICATION

Build a climate with your children where they can tell you anything. This means you let them finish without interruption or explosion. Always affirm that you love them unconditionally. I still tell my children, "I love you." I still kiss them on the cheek or the neck, as well as embrace them. I let them know early on that they did not have a bigger cheerleader than me. I believe beyond "I love you," the greatest words a dad can say to his children are the words, "I believe in you." This has built into my children the desire to talk with me almost every day. I still tell them, "I believe in you."

Communicate with the church about your children on a limited basis. I never lifted my children up because I felt it put them under the microscope even more. In fact, it was not until recently that I even taught on parenting because I did not want them under the gun. If I did, I qualified it first. I limited illustrations about them in my speaking because it just heightened the scrutiny. Please be wise in these areas. Your people will resent you and your children if you talk about them too much publicly and privately. Let another's words bring praise to them.

VALUE VACATIONS

Time away through the year is valuable to your family. In those early years, it was limited due to finances. I believe it is also important that as your children grow up you ensure that every vacation is not going to be spent with other family. They need time with you away from others.

We established in those early years the Floyd Family Fun Fund! The boys were laughing about it recently. Anytime I realized any "extra money," we placed it into this account. Why? In order that we could have a vacation that was away and as nice as resources would permit.

We attempted to go away on Spring Break week, one week in the summer, and usually the week between Christmas and New Year's. The summer trip was usually our biggest trip that we saved for and looked forward to the most. Spring Break was usually with a church group skiing in Colorado, and Christmas time we would spend with family.

Your children are not always going to be a part of your daily life. Therefore, while you have your children at home, value vacations. Remember in your marriage (meaning you had better take care of business in that relationship), your children will leave one day and you will be left with only your spouse. That will be great if your relationship with your spouse is healthy. We have loved every stage of life and have attempted to make each one very positive.

ONE MORE TIME

Please understand that I do not live in a perfect world. We are not perfect and do not have perfect children or a perfect grandchild. However, what we do have is a healthy family, a family full of love and grace. We want to be together.

I believe this can occur for any minister and his family if he values the right things. Just one more time to set the record straight: *Building Your Family Is More Important Than Building Your Church!* It is only possible by God's grace, prayer, and a lot of hard work. You will never regret doing it, so build your family!

Remember: *"If anyone does not know how to manage his own household, how will he take care of God's church?"* (1 Tim. 3:5).

5

YOU'RE NOT THINKING BIG ENOUGH

MY FIRST PASTORATE WAS IN A town of 300 people. Approximately 50 people attended the First Baptist Church when I arrived, give or take a family or two each week. It was a very special church. Each Sunday I would go to lunch at a different member's home. We will never forget those days. It was a great place for me to learn.

One of the greatest lessons about vision I learned in the simplest manner while I was at that church. Some of the church's leadership determined we needed to air condition the building. This led to a business meeting. We were discussing the situation as the ping-pong match began. One of the men felt strongly we did not need to do it because "times were hard." A godly woman in the church had heard about all she wanted to hear. She stood up and said to them, "God will take care of this. Let's help the church move forward to the future for our younger families." In her passionate speech and plea, she nailed the hard times issue by telling them she would give the first $1,000. To the best of my knowledge, that paid for almost one-third of the job. Needless to say, within minutes the whole issue was solved. The church was getting its own central heat and air unit.

In the middle of the match, I had resolved that the deal was over and that man had won again. However, I learned that night I was not thinking big enough! I had forgotten the power of vision and how people love to rally to a better future. The lady had called people to a better future, even demonstrating sacrifice toward it.

What God etched in my heart that night I will never forget. A godly lady had a vision and was not going to let anyone torpedo it. She had her sight set on younger families wanting to come to the church once it was

> I HAD FORGOTTEN THE POWER OF VISION AND HOW PEOPLE LOVE TO RALLY TO A BETTER FUTURE.

modernized with central heat and air. She was right. She painted a vision, and people ran toward it.

The Lord has used the lessons I learned that night and built upon them church by church and situation by situation. God wanted to build me into a man of vision and faith.

When I came to my present church in 1986 and preached for the church to vote on me becoming their pastor, I was grilled with questions for a long time in a gymnasium, the place we met for worship at that time. That night, I began to cast a vision in many areas.

I remember saying to them, "If God can use Wal-Mart to place retail stores all over the world from Northwest Arkansas, J.B. Hunt Transport to place trucks all over the world from Northwest Arkansas, Tyson Foods to place chickens all over the world from Northwest Arkansas, and the University of Arkansas to place Razorbacks all over the world from Northwest Arkansas, then surely He wants to use our church to place Jesus and His gospel all over the world from Northwest Arkansas." That was a strong statement of vision and faith. On that night, I rallied people to a better future.

Through the years, I felt there was no way that would happen, but I continued on in the vision. With the limited population in this region, I lost my vision and faith periodically. Sometimes I would believe we had peaked and there was no way for growth to continue. Yet it continued to happen. Every time I felt the lid was on, God would blow the lid off of the church. I was not thinking big enough! Each time I would look back and say to myself, "I should have known God better than that." Each time, vision and faith were contributing factors. Each time, people were rallying to a better future for their lives and our church.

Through a defining moment on January 4 of this year, God reinvented the vision I had shared on that day in 1986 about taking the gospel to the entire world from Northwest Arkansas. I believe a major part of the vision was fulfilled when the Lord miraculously opened the door for us to preach the good news of Jesus via daily television around the world, potentially into every country of the world. In January, this door did not exist, but God honored the vision I declared due to Him speaking to me through His Word. Therefore, in April of this year, we began to share God's good news daily around the world right here from Northwest Arkansas! You know, I have become convinced of one thing: *I am usually not thinking big enough!*

The vision has yet to be fulfilled because God keeps expanding it. There is so much more God wants to do! I am confident this is true for you, regardless of what size your town or church may be. It is the size of your vision that matters, nothing else.

> WHEN JESUS WAS ABOUT TO ASCEND TO BE WITH HIS FATHER IN HEAVEN, HE DEMONSTRATED THE BIG IDEA. IT ALL FIT INTO HIS EXTRAORDINARY PLAN. HE HAD DIED FOR OUR SINS. HE HAD BEEN RAISED FROM THE DEAD SUPERNATURALLY.

Vision is rallying people to a better future. Vision is helping people see what you see already. Vision is calling the invisible into visibility. Vision is usually determined by your burden and by your faith.

JESUS THINKS BIG!

When Jesus was about to ascend to be with His Father in heaven, He demonstrated the big idea. It all fit into His extraordinary plan. He had died for our sins. He had been raised from the dead supernaturally. Moments before His ascension, He laid some major visionary plans upon His faithful followers. He stated, as recorded by Luke in Acts 1:8:

But you will receive power when the Holy Spirit has come upon you, and you will be My witnesses in Jerusalem, in all Judea and Samaria, and to the ends of the earth.

This was a big idea. Jesus was thinking big! He was calling His followers to expand their belief in Him and His good news. He wanted His followers to begin sharing where they lived, then stretch to their own country, and eventually go into the entire world. This plan for reaching the world with news about His gift of eternal life became the marching orders to the church from our commander-in-chief, Jesus Christ. Any vision we have needs to be a vision that is tied to the vision of Jesus. He pulls for your vision to be fulfilled when you join Him in fulfilling His vision for the entire world, beginning with your own world.

When we do this, we experience a better future. We see things happen that do not logically make sense. We begin to realize that when God factors into our lives and churches, He creates something that is powerful! The supernatural power of God is unleashed upon you and your church when you have the heart for and begin to step toward reaching your region with the good news of Jesus with great intentionality. The power escalates along with the vision. It becomes the wind that soars your vision beyond what you have ever thought or imagined it to be.

Whether you are trusting God for central heat and air to be placed in your building, for preaching the gospel of Jesus world-wide every day on television, or something in between, ensure the vision somehow connects with reaching others for Jesus. When you connect what you desire to do with His vision, you send your vision to an entirely different level. The commitment from the divine toward you and your church begins to escalate.

Any vision you have must involve the One who thinks big. You cannot outthink Jesus. When your faith is frail, you are not thinking like Him. When your faith is timid, you are not thinking big enough.

Are you thinking big enough? Is your church thinking big enough? Is the ministry in which you are serving thinking big enough? It all begins with our vision. What is your vision to rally your people to a better future? Do you have one?

Receiving a Vision

A vision is beyond a good idea. It must be a God idea. God does not obligate himself to your good ideas or brainstorming sessions. He commits himself to you when you connect with His heart and vision for your world. He expands your vision as you begin to touch your world. No one is more committed to reaching your world than Jesus.

Therefore, get with Him. Hang out with Him. Ask Him what He wants you to do. If you have any element of desperation or sense of urgency, retreat with Him, entering into days of prayer and fasting. Get yourself to the point spiritually where you can hear what He is saying.

God began to redefine the vision in a new way for me on January 4, the day I shared with you a few moments ago. He used the passage from Habakkuk 2:1–4 to rivet my heart. This passage gives us five principles about vision:

* *Vision Given: God alone gives the vision.*
* *Vision Written: Write down what God is saying to you.*
* *Vision Declared: Communicate by faith what God has put into your heart.*
* *Vision Faithed: Trust God via prayer until He fulfills it.*
* *Vision Realized: If God says it, in time He will do it!*

Vision is not duplicating what He is doing with someone else. It will be crafted by God using your giftedness, packaging it into your culture. Once you have it written down, pray it every day. It is powerful and keeps you on course. If you do not write it, you or others cannot run to it. Sooner or later, you are going to have to step into the water and declare it. It does not take faith to declare what God has done visibly, but it does take faith to say verbally what God has reported to you He would like to do through you and your church.

What if you fail? What if it does not happen? Hear what God is saying to you through His Word. Write it down. Declare it verbally when He permits you to do so. Wait in faith. God is the one who brings it to reality, not you. When the "what ifs" dominate you, you are not thinking big enough!

CASTING A VISION

Casting a vision involves sharing it in all kinds of ways with all kinds of people, all for the purpose of helping them see what you see. I love to cast vision to people. Even though my knees may be knocking, I love to stand with the confidence of God's Word, step into the water, and rally the people to launch into that water with me.

I could tell you so many stories of how we have cast our vision through the years to our people. It takes hard work, much research, great teamwork, and various stages of meetings as you walk it through your organization before you make it known publicly. If the processes have been followed, it enables you to cast the vision to your people with confidence.

Beginning with the very first person or group you share it with, follow these vision-casting guidelines:

Cast it clearly: Above everything else, a leader must be clear.

Cast it simply: Keep it simple if you want them to grasp it.

Cast it visually: Technology is a friend to vision casting.

Cast it biblically: Tie the vision in to how it fulfills reaching others for Jesus.

Cast it creatively: God and others can help you do this.

Cast it enthusiastically: Passionate enthusiasm always attracts people to a better future.

When you follow these guidelines with the confidence that this is God's vision for you and your church, then people and resources will rally toward the better future you have promised them. Is it possible? Absolutely! You're not thinking big enough!

WALKING THE VISION

What does it mean to make the vision walk? So many leaders fumble the ball at this level. Walking the vision occurs when you follow the necessary steps to see the vision become a reality. You walk the vision through various people and processes so that the vision can be fulfilled. Some pay the price to get the vision, but do not take the time to walk the vision. Therefore, it is forfeited on the failure of the principle of follow-through.

> WALKING THE VISION OCCURS WHEN YOU FOLLOW THE NECESSARY STEPS TO SEE THE VISION BECOME A REALITY. YOU WALK THE VISION THROUGH VARIOUS PEOPLE AND PROCESSES SO THAT THE VISION CAN BE FULFILLED.

What does it take for something to come to reality in your church? The answer to this is different for each church. No church operates like another. The minister and his team of ministers or lay leaders must understand the culture enough to take the time to do what is necessary to walk the vision all the way through to see it come to a reality. If you have received the vision and have taken the time to create the presentation by the guidelines I gave for casting the vision, then you are ready to walk it through the various people and groups to ensure its success. Yes, this involves time and sacrifice. You may be thinking, *I cannot do that.* You're not thinking big enough!

When I look back on my ministry at this stage of life, there are only a few visions I know the Lord put into my heart that have failed. They are the ones I did not cast properly or did not take the time to walk once God gave me not only the vision, but also the way to cast it. Thank God I have not suffered that disappointment in a long time. It breaks my heart to think about the things God would have done if only I had taken the necessary time and steps to nurture and walk the vision through the necessary processes. As leaders, we cannot forfeit what God puts into our hearts because of over-enthusiasm, desperation, or just not wanting to pay the price to walk the vision. Most visions die and now lie in the spiritual carnage of our disappointments because we have not taken the necessary steps to walk the vision into a state of reality.

In our most recent financial campaign for campus expansion and growth, it took us three years to come up with the product to communicate. Once we had that, it took two months of my time to meet with various leaders before I went to the church publicly. Once I went to the church publicly, it took eight weeks to communicate the vision through all of the venues, plus an estimated 40 home meetings or larger venue meetings where I shared the vision. The financial campaign I led personally by this process was by far the most successful in our history and continues to be so. May God be praised!

Place this into your context, packaged with your giftedness. God wants to do it through you, whatever "it" is. God wants to do it wherever you are, wherever "wherever" is.

You can do it. You can do it where you are. You can think big enough. With God, all things are possible. You have to believe. You have to act upon that belief with wisdom.

Remember that God will run to you when you are communicating His vision. He will mobilize the forces and resources of heaven to verify what is on His heart that He has placed upon your heart.

FULFILLING THE VISION

There is nothing more exhilarating to a leader than when the vision is realized. It is a confirmation the leader has heard from God, cast God's heart in the right manner, and prayed it through as he walked it into reality.

At every church I have ever served, I could tell you stories of how I have experienced this fulfillment. Perhaps the methods have changed and the visions may have become larger in human scope, but their fulfillment comes down to the reality of those principles I shared with you from Habakkuk. Their fulfillment has come because the transfer has been made from God to me to the leaders to the church as the vision was received, was cast before God's people, and time was taken to walk it through into reality.

Any vision you see fulfilled is not a testimony about you and your ability, intellect, visionary capacity, organizational acumen, or people skills. If you believe any or all of those things were your secret to success, then you're not thinking big enough! God uses all of those things along the way and they are necessary, but God can use anyone. He used Balaam's donkey! Right? You should already be doing what you can do on your own!

Vision fulfilled is a testimony of a great God who enables you to think like Him. God is attracted to a people who rely on Him so strongly that without Him the vision is impossible. If you can do it on your own, then it is not a vision from God. You're not thinking big enough!

A Testimony

If you hold this book in your hand, it is probable that we are nearing or have even passed the time when a vision God had given me has been realized. This vision began in my heart seven years ago. It was a vision to expand our church and its reach with an additional location. The work has been going on very successfully for five years. However, in the fall of 2006, we will enter the first phase of buildings on this new campus.

My points are simple. Praise be to God alone. Vision takes time. It is worth it. You cannot out-think God. Think big!

Remember: *"For nothing will be impossible with God"* (Luke 1:37).

6

NOT EVERY HILL
IS WORTH DYING ON

THE GREATEST THING IN leadership I have learned in my 30 years of leading churches is: *Not every hill is worth dying on.* It took me many years to learn this. If I had learned it earlier in pastoral ministry, each church I have served would have prospered more effectively. The fellowship would have been sweeter, the growth would have been greater, and the preservation of that growth would have been more successful.

When did I learn the lesson? It did not happen at a turning point, but through a process. Some things in leadership you can only learn through your own growth and the growth of the entity you are assigned to lead. The evolving of the organization with growth in structures, personnel, dollars, and expectations requires the leader to operate by the conviction that not every hill is worth dying on.

As I write these words, I think about the times I could have carried so many more people along with me on the vision path if I had only been more patient and personal along the way.

In the name of "urgency" or "reaching," we can at times hurry matters in a church when hurrying up is not an asset, but a liability. Even though I believe I have operated with this principle in mind for the past decade, at this point I cannot go back and change things from earlier days. I must trust the sovereignty of God in all of it because blessings were more than apparent in each church I have served.

I cannot recall anyone telling me, "Ronnie, not every hill is worth dying on." I wish someone had spoken to me that clearly and directly. Perhaps they did, but my passion distorted my hearing. In case no one has said that to you, whether you are a rookie minister or an icon minister, let me tell you right now: *Not every hill is worth dying on.*

IT'S NOT ABOUT BEING RIGHT

Ministers are strong people. I believe God made us this way because He wants us to be strong as leaders, strong through conflict, and strong in engaging the culture. Yet the call from Jesus' heart is for us to be gentle. Gentle, not indicating weakness, but operating with tamed strength.

Most Christians are more interested in being right than they are about being Christ-like. When we always have to have our way or have the last word in a debate over an

> MINISTERS ARE STRONG PEOPLE. I BELIEVE GOD MADE US THIS WAY BECAUSE HE WANTS US TO BE STRONG AS LEADERS, STRONG THROUGH CONFLICT, AND STRONG IN ENGAGING THE CULTURE. YET THE CALL FROM JESUS' HEART IS FOR US TO BE GENTLE.

issue, we may lose people on the vision path because we do not operate with Christ-likeness. As ministers, we can add to the fire at times, rather than serving as the vessel of peace in the midst of the storm.

Wounded Christians lay on the brink of becoming spiritual carnage on the side streets of our churches because a minister or an employee or a church leader "just had to be right." Someone just had to make a point. Someone did not have the wisdom to let it go, but stayed on it too long to bring lasting benefit.

The Christian life is not about being right. It is about being Christ-like. I heard this said years ago and I have never forgotten it: *If Satan cannot get you to do the wrong thing, he will get you to do the right thing in the wrong way.* This satanic ploy has limited, jeopardized, or ruined many ministers.

When you think you always have to be right, you will have to die on needless hills. Being right and being Christ-like do not have to be competing forces. Rightness is doing something the way Jesus would do it. Jesus not only did what was right, but He always did it in the right way. He was a picture of godliness and holiness, and He brought glory to God the Father.

Do not lose your testimony over being right. Do not lose your leadership over being right. Add to your testimony and your leadership by being Christ-like. This takes care of both at once.

Each time you make a decision, you either add to the value of your account or you lose value on your account. What is your leadership value right now in your church?

What's in Your Pocket?

Years ago, at a leadership conference conducted by former pastor and now leadership guru John Maxwell, I heard him talk about "the change in your pocket." I may not remember all the details, but I have never forgotten the basic principle.

A leader has only so much change in his pocket. Your calling gives you some change. Your position gives you some change. Your tenure gives you some change. Years ago, church leaders started with a lot of change in their pocket. People used to respect the call of God upon a person's life, far more than they do today. People used to respect the position of the pastor far more than they do today. People used to respect tenure in a given ministry far more than they do today. So as a minister today, you start with less change in your pocket than any generation of ministers before you.

Therefore, the change you have in your pocket this very moment based upon your calling, position, and tenure can only be increased through proper decision-making. Conversely, since you have only so much change in your pocket to begin with, and since you may have lost a little due to some decisions made, you lose more change when you do not make good decisions.

When you constantly have to prove you are right and don't take time to work toward making the best decision at the right time, you will lose more change in your pocket. If this occurs and you face a hill that you have to die on, you will have nothing left in your pocket to go to a committee, a board, a body, a group, or even to an individual to ask them to join you in your desired vision path.

> **THE CHANGE YOU HAVE IN YOUR POCKET THIS VERY MOMENT BASED UPON YOUR CALLING, POSITION, AND TENURE CAN ONLY BE INCREASED THROUGH PROPER DECISION-MAKING.**

It is my goal as a leader to be loaded with change in both of my pockets. It should be your goal, also. This does not mean you do nothing. If you think that, you have missed it completely. What this means is that your wisdom in leadership exercised over time has resulted in ample change in your pocket. This way, not if, but when the hills come that you have to be willing to die on, you will have ample change to recover in your leadership.

Never underestimate the value of making an investment in people. I had a good friend, Jack Bailey, who was a crusty old football coach and a former Razorback. Jack had an enormous influence on the lives of both my boys. Jack could tell story after story, from his days in the military to recounting each game he coached. Jack so willingly cared for and loved others, especially the younger generation. I saw him do this again and again. Since Jack died, we have missed him so much.

I am convinced that one reason Jack always took a great interest in my boys, Josh and Nick, is because the first time I remember meeting him was after he had surgery. I was the new pastor in town, making the hospital rounds. I can still recall walking into that room to see this big man. There were tubes everywhere, but he was cracking jokes. When he found out I was a football lover, we connected immediately. You see, along the way in ministry life many years after this, whether it was his service or counsel

I needed about my boys, old Jack Bailey gave it willingly. Why? Because of my investment into his life in those opening ministry days. I gained change in my pocket to call upon him. The interesting thing is, so did he. I would have attempted to climb Mount Everest because of his investment into the lives of my boys!

I am living right now in the blessing of having change in my pocket that only comes through years of service to the same church. I am able to lead our fellowship to do things we would have not considered in years past. This is possible because of trust that only comes when you have change in your pocket. When you have led the same people for 20 years, they have witnessed your highest and lowest moments in life and ministry. When you are consistent, willing to admit your weaknesses and failures, as well as applaud them because of the successes, you add change in your pocket.

THE HILLS WORTH DYING ON

Some of you will be relieved to know that I do believe there are some hills worth dying on. In this day and time, there are plenty, but let's focus in on just three of them.

Truth

I must be willing to die on the hill of God's truth found in Scripture. The Bible is God's infallible Word. It not only contains the Word of God, but it *is* the Word of God. The Bible is truth without any mixture of error. I am a Christian minister who believes in the inerrancy of Scripture, yet I believe we should only defend it in Christ-likeness.

More people are more willing to die for their traditions than for the truth found in Holy Scripture. When the Bible is mocked or scorned, we must be willing to die on that hill. You must stand in your pulpits, in your meetings, and everywhere else you go with the confidence that the Bible is God's truth for today.

Therefore, the Scripture, nothing else, should navigate what churches do. Scripture is not threatened by someone packaging it in creativity as long as Scripture remains the focus. Orthodoxy can be packaged in innovation. This does not jeopardize truth. It verifies that truth is eternal. It verifies that truth can stand the test of time.

Therefore, you must have enough change in your pockets that when someone in your church wants to question the virgin birth of Jesus or they are standing in

> WHEN THE BIBLE IS MOCKED OR SCORNED, WE MUST BE WILLING TO DIE ON THAT HILL. YOU MUST STAND IN YOUR PULPITS, IN YOUR MEETINGS, AND EVERYWHERE ELSE YOU GO WITH THE CONFIDENCE THAT THE BIBLE IS GOD'S TRUTH FOR TODAY.

a classroom or leading a study questioning that it is truly grace alone that saves, you can stand up for what the Bible teaches and have people rally with you wholeheartedly. The result will be that you will have more coins in your leadership pockets than you had when you began to deal with the issue.

Morality

Jesus was very clear about the church being salt and light in this world. We must be the moral conscience of our regions, nation, and world. Biblically, we have no alternative. We have to engage the culture.

Therefore, in this fragmented society inside and outside of the church, we may be challenged when we have to stand for righteousness in matters pertaining to the hot button issues in our world. Ministers have to live morally upright and we need to hold the standard high in our churches and in our nation.

Consider the present-day marriage debate — do we have a choice on taking a stand? We must stand for one man being married to one woman for a lifetime. It is not about two men living together or two women living together in unholy matrimony. If we do not stand strong for biblical marriage, we are contributing to the efforts of those who want to redefine marriage. The one place people must hear God's truth is the church.

Therefore, you will spend some change with a few people when you speak out in the marriage debate, but you will lose a lot of change with others if you decide to sit on the bench during moral debates. Our mission is to change the world with the life-changing message of Jesus Christ. This must always remain central, not the social issues of our day. We will have to speak to the challenges along the way or we will end up with a very mediocre commitment to morality in our churches.

By the way, let's understand clearly. These issues are biblical issues, not moral issues. Keep the debate on what God says. Stay on the message of what the Bible says. When you speak about God's truth, you always represent what is right; however, let's remember that we must always do so in a Christ-like manner.

Great Commission

The Great Commission (Matt. 28:19) should drive every Christian and every church. The Great Commission is Jesus' command to make disciples in every people group in the world, "baptizing them . . . teaching them." Every Christian needs to be a Great Commission Christian who is an active part of a Great Commission church.

For a church to advance toward the future in health and growth, the church needs to be emblazoned by the Great Commission. Yet not everyone involved in church shares a passion to have a healthy and growing church with the world on its heart. I have always been told that people in church will be happy until you ask them to serve, ask them to give, and ask them to go. Serving, giving, and sending are all part of being a Great Commission church. Herein lies the challenge of leading a church toward fulfilling their God-assigned task.

How much change do you have in your pocket? I hope you have some to spend on ensuring your church moves toward the fulfillment of your assignment. When you ask people to die to their own dreams for the sake of unity in the church, it may cost you. When you ask people to become equipped in special ways, it may cost you. When you ask people to serve and step up to greater service and commitment, it may cost you. When you ask people to give of the resources God has given to them, it may cost you. When you ask people to go into their own world and the multiple people groups all around the world to share Jesus, it may cost you. All of this and more should come as a strong conviction about and commitment to the Great Commission.

There are other matters through life and leadership that are hills you may need to die on. I have just chosen these three because they seem to be quite dominant in our culture, even church culture, today.

When You Go To the Hill

Good leadership determines not only to die on the right hills, but chooses the timing of when to ascend the hills for battle. Let's mention some strategic experiences you should go through before you ascend the hill.

Leadership has been clear

There are many voices in today's world competing with your voice as a minister and leader. What you live as the leader may be lived only an hour to a few hours a week by your people. What appears to be clear to you may still be unclear to them. The competing voices can get you in trouble if you assume your people are hearing what you are saying. One of the biggest sins of church leadership is the sin of assumption. We cannot assume anything. We must be clear.

If you have been clear and the people can articulate back to you the issue at hand, then leadership has been clear. If that is so, then you move on to ensure that the . . .

Processes have been thorough

When the leadership has been clear, you need to ensure the processes have been thorough. Have you gone through the various networks of decision-making bodies on the issue at hand? Have you done your homework? Have you connected with the right players about the matter at hand to answer their questions or address their concerns?

These questions, as well as others, are important to answer in order to ensure the processes have been clear. You cannot get yourself into trouble or lose an important biblical, moral, or Great Commission decision because you did not take the time to walk the issue through the processes in your unique church culture.

If the leadership has been clear and the processes have been thorough, then one of the most important and final experiences is in regard to . . .

God's timing

Before you ascend the hill, you need to check the timing. The decision to ascend the hill cannot be made because of pressure from a special interest group in the church or because you would just like to get the matter behind you. It has to be God's timing. When God's timing is right and you stand for truth, morality, or the Great Commission, the chances of winning at the hill are greatly enhanced. Yet remember, all of these three may occur and you may still lose at the hill with many, most, or all of the people.

Wisdom is exercised when you have been clear and know it, the processes have been thorough, and you have waited on God's timing to ascend the hill. A wise man will always do things in

God's timing in God's way by God's Word. If you have worked through these issues and you stand in confidence, you have no other choice other than to ascend the hill.

WRAP-UP

Do not die on needless hills. You will have to die on a few necessary hills as a leader. Just make sure when you do that you have some change left in your leadership pockets. Don't waste your change on matters of insignificance in the big picture of church and leadership — matters like colors for a room, furniture preferences, having to have the final word about something within a committee, what you need to do at one of the Christmas services, or whether the parking lot needs to be paved now or three months from now. Keep the big picture. Choose your hills wisely.

From one minister to another: *Not every hill is worth dying on.*

Remember: "He has made everything appropriate in its time" (Eccles. 3:11).

7

RELATIONSHIPS
MOVE YOUR MINISTRY

I AM CONVINCED THAT LEADING people is about influencing their lives. Influence is about putting your spiritual brand on and in people. People matter to God. Therefore, people should matter to you.

If your mode of operation comes with the cynical view represented in the following statement, then your influence will be limited dramatically: *"The ministry would be great if it were not for people."* If you believe that in any level or at any capacity, then you are in for a long, isolated, and lonely ministry journey.

Influencing people in the 21st century will not occur just because of your position, giftedness, style, training, experience, or even success. Influencing people in our generation will come because you have a relationship with them. You must be as personal as possible and create the perception of being a relational leader.

Relationships move your ministry. Relationships build the church. Relationships move the church forward. Relationships move the gospel. Relationships are essential to fulfill the mission.

Love travels on the tracks of a relationship. This means genuine agape love can only happen through having a relationship with others. Since people matter to God and they should matter to you, love is the way you indent their lives. This only comes through having a genuine relationship with them.

In this cynical world where suspicion exists about anyone who is in a place of leadership and influence, having relationships is the only way you can counter this skepticism. Again, this means you must be as personal as possible and create the perception of being a relational leader. This will help limit the influence of skeptics and cynics toward those of us in authority.

MAXIMIZING YOUR INFLUENCE

There are a couple of statements I want to introduce to you that are glaring realities existent today. I hope you will take time to digest them. I want you to meditate on them and I pray you will act on them.

> *Statement #1: If you are going to influence people toward a common goal, you must have a relationship with them.*

You can be the president of Wal-Mart or Microsoft, the head football coach of the University of Texas or the Dallas Cowboys, the president of the United States, the governor of Georgia, or the pastor of Saddleback Church or First Christian of Slippery Rock; however, you will not influence people toward a common goal without having a relationship with them. There is not one leader or minister in the world who can escape this principle in the 21st century. You must be a person who connects with people.

Some of you are entrusted with the responsibility and blessing of having one staff member on your team or several staff members on your team. Some of you *are* these staff members. When any of you ask others to join your team or you have been asked to join a team, unite with someone who understands and connects with people. If a person today does not attract and go after people, then that person cannot move others to a common goal.

> YOU CAN BE THE PRESIDENT OF WAL-MART OR MICROSOFT, THE HEAD FOOTBALL COACH OF THE UNIVERSITY OF TEXAS OR THE DALLAS COWBOYS, THE PRESIDENT OF THE UNITED STATES, THE GOVERNOR OF GEORGIA, OR THE PASTOR OF SADDLEBACK CHURCH OR FIRST CHRISTIAN OF SLIPPERY ROCK; HOWEVER, YOU WILL NOT INFLUENCE PEOPLE TOWARD A COMMON GOAL WITHOUT HAVING A RELATIONSHIP WITH THEM.

Could it be that many of our dreams in church fail at this point? Could it be that we just do not want to take the time or make the sacrifices necessary to create, nurture, and build relationships? It takes time, making yourself accessible, and intentionality to do this in life. Maximizing your influence means that you make relationships high on your agenda.

Statement #2: Ministry leadership is all about relationships.

People will not care about you and the church until they know you care. As you take time to build your relational skills, take time to pray that God gives you genuine care for people. Jesus was moved and overcome with compassion for others. Ministry cannot be heartless and be ministry. Ministry is about people, people, and more people.

If you want to lead them, you have to relate to them. If you want to take them with you toward the fulfillment of taking the good news of Jesus in your region, nation, and world, you are going to have to relate to them. If you want them to support a project or an event of some kind, you are going to have to relate to them. Connecting with people is a part of maximizing your leadership.

The most effective staff players on our staff team are those who understand the power of connecting with others. Their ministries grow and, guess what, people love them. Love is reciprocal. You have to give love via relationships if you want love demonstrated back to you. Maximize your leadership by connecting with others.

PAUL, A PEOPLE CONNECTOR

Have you ever wondered why the apostle Paul was so successful in advancing the gospel? You really should ask that question. If you study it, here is what you find.

Read what Luke says about Paul in the Book of Acts. Read the letters from Paul that he wrote to the churches. Read Romans 16 and, by the way, read slowly. Do not just race through the names he mentions. These names represent real people. Do not speed past what he says about these people. He is giving you his secret of how he moved the gospel.

> LOVE IS RECIPROCAL. YOU HAVE TO GIVE LOVE VIA RELATIONSHIPS IF YOU WANT LOVE DEMONSTRATED BACK TO YOU.

Paul advanced the gospel through relationships. He related to doctors, lawyers, private business people, politicians, plain people, intellectual people, religious people, non-religious people, and influential people, as well as pastors, Christian leaders, and churches. Paul connected with people. He understood the secret of moving and advancing the gospel. He knew it only happened by influencing people.

Paul is so misunderstood by some people. Paul had a heart as big as New York City, even though his message was as narrow as one of the alley streets there. Paul understood people. Paul understood that he could maximize his influence as a Christian leader through relationships. We need to understand and influence people as he did through his heart, passion, and strategy.

LIMITING YOUR INFLUENCE

You limit your influence when you do not relate well to people. This could happen because of bad habits in your life. Family is our school on relationships. Sometimes influence is limited because you are insecure or extremely shy. Other times, it may be limited because of past actions with people that they will just never forget.

You limit your influence when you have no interest in people. I have heard of ministers who are just never accessible to people.

Some are out the side or back door the moment they step away from the pulpit on Sundays or complete their job responsibilities. Others do nothing to show they are real people themselves. Still others just never care about anyone but themselves.

If this is the way you operate, you are in for one unfulfilling ministry. Your impact will be like a drop of water landing in the Atlantic Ocean. Why in the world are you in ministry if you do not want to relate to people?

A STRATEGIC THOUGHT

Since you are on assignment by Jesus Christ to reach your city, I have a strategic thought for you to consider. I realize the challenge of leadership in a church. I realize what a busy schedule is like. I realize what it is like to go strong for 16–18 hours a day, several days in a row, and still your list is growing. I know you cannot relate to everyone personally, regardless of the size of your church. One thing you must determine is to connect with the people in your fellowship who influence other people.

Here is my strategic thought: *Pray about initiating, developing, nurturing, and maintaining influential relationships that have potential to move the gospel.*

This does not mean that you only relate to a certain kind of person who has a certain kind of influence and happens to have a certain kind of bank account. A minister relates to all people. However, a minister only has so much time with the demands upon his life. Therefore, you need to ensure that the time you spend on relationships is spent influencing others who can help influence the gospel in the greatest way in your region. If you do not do this, you will limit the advancement of the gospel as well as your leadership.

There are some people in your church you will never engage in advancing the gospel unless you invest in their lives. You may be the only one who can get them to partner with you and your church to take the good news of Jesus to the entire world. Some people will only be equipped by you. Some will only be motivated by you toward spiritual growth. Some will only let you add value to and influence their lives. This is another reality that exists whether you recognize it or not.

Oh, by the way, there are some people in your region that only you can reach for Christ. You can create a relationship with them through a note, a call, a lunch, or just by telling them you want to hear what is going on in their life. You have watched and appreciated their leadership. Therefore, whether it is 20 minutes or 60 minutes, get to know them. Find common ground. Go slowly. Enter their world first, if you ever want them to enter your world spiritually.

> HERE IS MY STRATEGIC THOUGHT: PRAY ABOUT INITIATING, DEVELOPING, NURTURING, AND MAINTAINING INFLUENTIAL RELATIONSHIPS THAT HAVE POTENTIAL TO MOVE THE GOSPEL.

In time, you may have the opportunity at just the right moment to influence them, introducing them to Jesus Christ personally. I have had lunches with business powerbrokers, sports icons, socialites, medical community leaders, real estate developers, politicians, and others, none of whom went to my church.

To their great surprise, I entered their world, even though they do not operate in my world, and did not ask them for one thing. I just wanted to get to know them. However, I did it because I care about them, the region I have been called to serve and reach, and because I know it is in the heart of Jesus for Ronnie Floyd to relate to other people.

I hope you will consider this strategic thought I have just given to you. I believe it will move the gospel and your ministry beyond your imagination.

IDEAS

I want to give you some ideas to consider in relating to others personally. Some may help create the perception that you are more personal, even though time may not permit you to spend personal time with each person to get to know them.

In the early churches I served, I visited everyone in the church intentionally, strategically, and periodically. I went to several hospitals in one day and the closest was 15 miles away. Yes, I used to spend all day at several hospitals or in the car making all the stops, not once a week, but daily. I even used to know all the people by name. There are days I yearn to return to that life because I love people and want to pastor them personally and genuinely. However, things have changed in my life, in my church, and in our culture. I just cannot be all things to all people. I have only so much time and energy.

Regardless of the size of your church, some of the ideas I want to suggest for you to consider may assist you in moving your ministry and the gospel forward via relationships.

Accessibility

People want to know, "If I called my pastor's office and needed to talk to him personally, would he talk to me? If I sent him an e-mail, would he read it and respond to it?" People want to know you are accessible. It is always powerful to tell stories of what God is doing in the lives of others. It shows that you are approachable and accessible.

Hang out after church. Jeana and I still go outside on Sunday mornings to greet people following our final service. We love doing it. I tell the people, "I will be in the back if you need to see me." If we are doing Sunday night church, I hang out down front. Most of the time, Jeana and I are close to the last ones to leave, if not the last ones to leave the worship center. The people know where you are. They know they can come up and talk with you even if they do not. They see you visiting with others or praying with others. Do not let some of the "challenging members" in your congregation dominate that time or discourage you from just hanging out. Expend yourself on Sunday. Your people have limited time just like you do. Invest your Sundays in people while they have more time.

On a typical Sunday, I get up no later than 4:00 a.m. I pray and go over the message for at least 75 minutes. I exercise on Sunday mornings for 40 minutes. Then I go and prepare myself for the day. I am at the church by 7:50 a.m. I then briefly ensure I understand my responsibilities for the day. I retreat to my study for final prayer and preparation for 40 minutes. I walk downstairs at 8:45 a.m. and enter a room where a group of men are already praying for me. They lay hands on me and pray over me for a few minutes. I walk out and go throughout the worship center for five minutes greeting people. I then conduct the morning services at both campuses.

We usually have lunch with a couple, two or three families, or even a large meeting group. I get home by 2:30 or 3:00 p.m. if I do not have a television or media shoot. I may get a brief nap for quick refreshment. I then prepare myself again for the evening service if we are having it. Following the service, if we are in that season, I will usually go out to dinner with some people before going home. Therefore, Jeana and I may not be home until 9:00 p.m. And yes, I do work on Monday, bright and early.

Why do I want to spend my day off feeling drained? What is my point? Accessibility! My point is also that if you will expend yourself on Sunday, you will gain more time back in the week. Hanging out after services will save you time in correspondence or appointments in the week to come.

Transparency

Many years ago I read an article about the importance of being transparent when you preach. The call was to make yourself vulnerable. The point of the article was that you would only impact people in your communication to the point you were willing to share your personal journey with them of failure, disappointment, struggle, and even victory. I read that article somewhere in some magazine at least 25 years ago. Was it not cutting-edge? Transparency and authenticity is not new today.

The importance of sharing your journey in your communication is critical. Bragging is not acceptable and will be repelled by your people. I am talking about the importance of telling stories about yourself, your family, or experiences, especially when the stories let them see inside of you to see your failures or struggles in the faith. Of course, it is always good when you can laugh at yourself about something stupid you did or even tell a comical experience you had.

I told the story of a skunk one Sunday night at church and the people still talk about it. I told the story in a morning service of being in the worst Colorado blizzard in decades, driving in a rental car where the windshield wipers stopped working, resulting in Nick and me using his shoe laces to operate the windshield wipers manually to keep the ice and snow off of the windshield. He had seen the idea on television. God is sovereign. We did it! Needless to say, the people still talk about it.

If you come across as impersonal in the pulpit because you never let them inside of you and your heart, they will not be impacted by the message itself. Let the illustrations from your life honor God, accentuate a point you are trying to make, and limit talking about your successes or family successes. If you do this with wisdom, you will be believable by others when you communicate.

Technology

Internet technology has created avenues for communication for those of us in the people communication ministry. I use technology continuously.

E-mail has become an outstanding way to communicate with people in my church, on my staff team, as well as people around the world. Be careful and be wise, but it can be a great way to relate to others. Cell phone technology can give you 24/7 e-mail access as well as text messaging, which is huge to children and teenagers.

I would encourage you to collect and continue to collect all of the e-mail addresses of your members. I determined to do this after 9-11. I began doing this because I wanted to be able to have instant communication with our people over national issues or tragedies, as well as unique major church events or experiences in which I want to communicate with them directly and instantaneously. I promised we would not abuse it. I have to sign off for it to be used at all. I want to preserve the power of it so when they get an e-mail from me, it means something and they know it is important.

I began a blog in the fall of 2005. It is called *Between Sundays*. It is designed to share my life between the Sundays. The address is: www.betweensundays.com. Recently, a writer named Terry Wilhite with Rick Warren's "Pastors.com" recognized our blog as the leading blog by a pastor in America due to several of his criteria.

I blog four or five days a week. It takes me 20 minutes or so daily. I talk about family, what is going on in my life, schedule, challenges, and give prayer requests. I may do some lessons (but very few) and devotionalize rarely. I even give predictions on football games periodically. You can read about my grandson, Peyton, and even see updated pictures of him.

It is about the experiences of my life, so the people can get inside of me. Every day is different and will represent to some degree what is happening in my life. That is the point of blogging. My blog started just a couple of weeks before Hurricane Katrina. It gave me instantaneous access to our people, and we mobilized major money toward the disaster, as well as personnel and trips. God can use it in all kinds of ways.

It has been one of the most successful things I have done as a pastor to connect with my people. It makes them feel like they know me. If I blog well, they do know me. They know my heart. They know things about me most would not know.

Yes, blogging can get out of control. We attempt to have a more controlled environment. This website has become the second most popular site of all the ones we have as of now. Unique first-time visitors visit it continually. I am totally against any blog, but especially Christian blogs, where Christians slash other believers. It is ungodly and carnal, very much in violation of Scripture. Yet you can control that occurring, so do not let this discourage you. You will be shocked at the response you get when you announce to your people that you have created a blog.

You Can Be Personal

There are so many ways you can create your life and personality to be personal and authentic. Pray about becoming more relational as a minister. I am confident that Jesus will give you ways far beyond mine that will be appropriate for your personality and leadership style.

Remember: *"Give my greetings to Prisca and Aquila, my co-workers in Christ Jesus, who risked their own necks for my life. Not only do I thank them, but so do all the Gentile churches. Greet also the church that meets in their home"* (Rom. 16:3–5).

8

DECISION-MAKING IS NOT ABOUT YOU

A SURVEY WAS MADE BY *MSN Sidewalk Online Guide* about decision-making in the family. They discovered that Americans make an average of 73 decisions each day regarding work, purchases, home, and family. Men are more driven by technical, automotive, and career decisions. Women influence household matters, travel, family, and entertainment.

I wonder what this survey would look like if it were conducted with ministers and their families. In fact, I would be very curious to see what it would look like with ministers alone concerning their decision-making in their churches. I guarantee the results would be very interesting and the number of decisions made daily would escalate dramatically over the other survey.

The challenge of decision-making in ministry is the influence of the rising tides that surround us. We are pressured to make decisions due to specific situations. The persuasive argument is to make it relative to where you are in a given situation. We are pressured to make decisions due to our feelings. The pressure comes at this point both externally and internally, calling us to "feel" our way in decision-making. We are pressured to make decisions that will lead to the greatest results. Special interest groups within our churches push and shove us, attempting to intimidate us into getting involved in every issue that comes down the pipeline, all in the name of obtaining their own desired results pertaining to the issue at hand.

TWO FACTS

As ministers, we can get ourselves into some real trouble when we make our decisions in ministry based upon situations, feelings, or even desired results. There are two facts about decision-making in ministry that I want to share with you.

#1: Decision-making in ministry will only be right, consistent, and best when the decisions are made upon the basis of the authority of Scripture, God's Word, the Bible.

As ministers, we must be compelled to make decisions that are right, consistent, and best for everyone involved. Therefore, situations, feelings, and desired results cannot be the criteria. Decisions can only be right, consistent, and best when they are decisions that God desires.

These decisions must be based upon Scripture. A minister forfeits his right to make decisions based upon anything other than the authority of Scripture or by its principles for decision-making.

#2: Decision-making in ministry will only be harmonious when a common authority is agreed upon. This authority must be the Bible.

Decision-making cannot be driven by the will of a church member, a staff member, or even a pastor. Decision-making in ministry has to be driven by a common authority, which is Holy Scripture. When a church determines that Scripture will be the ultimate criteria for their decision-making, they set themselves up to be in agreement. They desire to do the will of God by the Word of God.

> AS MINISTERS, WE CAN GET OURSELVES INTO SOME REAL TROUBLE WHEN WE MAKE OUR DECISIONS IN MINISTRY BASED UPON SITUATIONS, FEELINGS, OR EVEN DESIRED RESULTS.

While situations, feelings, and desired results will be considered with great sensitivity and wisdom, our ultimate guiding star in decision-making must be the Bible. This is the map we must travel by in ministry and church life. If we do not follow Scripture as our ultimate guide, we will see some trouble along the way. However, if you want God on your side, you had better ensure you are on God's side. I would rather go down doing it God's way with His leadership, than go down trying to please or accommodate others and at the same time displease God.

It is very difficult to navigate your way through decision-making in ministry. Permitting the Bible to guide you will give you greater clarity in most areas. Moral, social, and many ministry decisions are somewhat easy and clear for us in the Bible. However, the challenges come in those day-to-day decisions in ministry in regards to calendar, budgeting, schedule, or even personnel. These may not always be found in the Bible with a chapter and verse, and principles may not pertain specifically to some of them.

THIS I KNOW

There is one thing I know with great conviction and passion concerning decision-making in the church: *Decision-making is not about you.* I believe it is imperative for a minister to believe this about making decisions in his ministry. If he does not, then wars and rumors of wars will occur continually.

Jesus has called us to be servant-leaders, not selfish-leaders. Jesus has called us to be willing to lay our lives down, not to take our lives up. We are called to sacrifice and death, not rights and declarations.

I want to ask you to always remember this: *Decision-making is not about you.* As you keep this in your heart, it will assist you and your church in various decisions that need to be made. As this becomes your passion and conviction, it helps as you evaluate and work through the matrix for decision-making in ministry.

> THERE IS ONE THING I KNOW WITH GREAT CONVICTION AND PASSION CONCERNING DECISION-MAKING IN THE CHURCH: DECISION-MAKING IS NOT ABOUT YOU.

THE MATRIX

Decisions about personnel, calendar, schedule,

budgeting, and some other things need to be processed. If the Bible does not speak to them with chapter and verse, what do you follow? Is there a matrix to follow in church or ministry decision-making? Is there anything that could make some of these "delicate decisions" easier? For several years, I have believed there is a matrix, form, mold, or grid to follow. Let me introduce to you the key and sequential questions to ask in the matrix for ministry decision-making. The order is significant and cannot be ignored.

Q 1: What is best for the church?

There are so many battles and skirmishes that could be eliminated if this first question was answered unselfishly and honestly. Since decision-making is not about you and since a local church or ministry employs you, this question should drive your decision-making. Jesus wants what is best for His church.

Best is determined by what is biblical and long term, not by what is personal and short term. Refuse to let the pressure of others or the delicate nature of the situation drive you away from what is best for the church.

The church needs to be protected from knowing all, but at times the church needs to be informed. Pertaining to matters of church discipline, this can become quite delicate, yet we have practiced church discipline at various levels with members and employees alike. We have even gone to the church on a Sunday morning to deal with an individual publicly. No, it was not easy, but the decision was made because we felt that in the long term, it was best for the church. Of course, church discipline at various levels is also biblical. The intention must be both to correct and to restore.

Concerning matters like budgeting, scheduling, personnel, and other similar things, this question should drive the decision process. What is best for the church is rather clear on most of these kinds of issues, unless silo thinking is occurring.

Silo thinking is when you contain your thinking in a particular cylinder of ministry. For example, if you believe God is leading you to do a financial campaign over a 60-day period of time, then having a major musical or pageant at the same time would not be wise. Therefore, what is best for the church? You cannot and should not do everything. There is nothing wrong with the pageant, musical, or the financial campaign. Yet if you have sensed God's leadership because long-term growth will be influenced by the building you need to build with the monies you are raising, then the pageant or musical may not fit into the church schedule this year. It does not mean it is bad or wrong, but it may not be best for the church at this time.

Silo thinking on a church staff team is detrimental. Silo thinking by various ministries cannot be permitted to exist. Silo thinking will eventually create division and strife.

Every pastor and minister on a staff team needs to teach the church and all of the various ministries the importance of this matrix. The first question of the matrix is most pivotal of all: What is best for the church? If it is biblical it is an easy choice, really not even a choice at all, because it is best for the church. If it is big-picture thinking rather than silo thinking, it is best for the church. If it is a long-term decision for the future of the church, it is better than a short-term, crowd-pleasing decision.

In the long term, the best for the church is always best for everyone associated with the church. A minister or lay person who cannot grasp the importance of this first question in the matrix will prove to be detrimental to the fellowship of the church.

Q 2: What is best for the office of the pastor?

If the decision has not been reached after the first matrix question has been addressed, then the next key question in the matrix is this: What is best for the office of the pastor? Why is this important? Is this not a little selfish? It is very important and not selfish at all.

The office of the pastor is the ministry office that serves the church. You will not find in the Bible the various staff minister titles we have today. This does not make them wrong, but it makes us ask, which are in the Bible? We know the pastor-teacher is a gift that operates the ministry of the local church. We know it has unique and distinct value. The Scripture esteems the office; therefore, we should esteem the office. Any staff member serves at the will of the pastor and is an extension of his calling as pastor-teacher of the church.

Let me make something very clear to you. I am not speaking of a particular or specific pastor; I am speaking of the office of the pastor. This is something much holier than a man.

In our nation, the office of the president is highly esteemed. While some presidents may be less popular with the American people than other presidents, this does not jeopardize the office of the president. One of the unique ideals in American government is the distinct value of the office of the president. When the media or fellow governmental workers or the American people demean the president, the office becomes jeopardized to a degree. If anyone would ever demean the office itself, a coup could occur in the land. America must never permit the office of the president to ever lose its esteem in any way.

A pastor is not a president, and you cannot compare the office of the pastor with the office of the president. One is a governmental office while the other is a spiritual office. My point is simple: Anytime the office of the pastor is jeopardized, demeaned, or lowly esteemed, you are on the brink of disaster in your church. Again, this is not about a man, but an office.

The pastors, staff ministers, and lay members must always work to esteem the office of the pastor. Compromise in any way will only lead to an unhealthy church and poor decision-making.

The matrix for decision-making in ministry begins with: What is best for the church? It continues with the question: What is best for the office of the pastor? If the decision has made it through these two pivotal questions, it now comes to the third criteria in the matrix.

Q 3: What is best for a specific ministry?

It may be best to use an illustration at this point of the matrix. Let's imagine that a student pastor desires his student camp to be moved this year to a different location and date. As he worked through the matrix with his supervisor, he knows where he has been going is just not best for the church. It was okay, but just not best per location or calendar. Therefore, he is changing to do what is best for the church.

With a great spirit, he has led the way in this transition. As he has navigated it through the proper matrix questions, he knows what may be best for the church may not be best for his ministry. In fact, most of those who had attended camp loved the location and time. Yet each summer it was a strain because of geographic location making the expense too big a factor for the greatest number of students to attend.

He also knows that what is best for the church will prove to be best for the office of the pastor. Additionally, his pastor had asked him to prayerfully consider a possible transition without destroying his own student ministry.

Since the matrix was established and worked through by a Spirit-controlled student pastor who understands it, he is transitioning the location of his camp because it is best for the church, and his pastor had requested him to prayerfully consider it. The student pastor understands that what is best for the church and the office of the pastor is always best in the long term for the success of his ministry.

With this illustration, do you understand the matrix and how it works? I hope so, because if you have established this matrix and operate by it, you will be blessed and cover a multitude of sins in the process.

Q 4: What is best for you?

In my 30 years of serving as a pastor of a church, this question in the matrix is usually the first one in the minds of pastors, staff ministers, and lay people. A "what is best for me" mindset destroys fellowship in the church every time it is exercised.

Ministry decision-making is not about you. It is about the Bible and what God says. It is about what is best for the church. It is about what is best for the office of the pastor. It is about what is best for your specific ministry. It is then about what is best for you.

When you return in your mind to the student pastor in the illustration I used a moment ago, perhaps the location for the camp or the new date was not his personal preference. Perhaps it was far away from his family or friends, yet he was willing to die to himself and his dreams.

The Outcome

This kind of humble spirit honors God. It also endears others to you. Trust me, it

> A "WHAT IS BEST FOR ME" MINDSET DESTROYS FELLOWSHIP IN THE CHURCH EVERY TIME IT IS EXERCISED.

always comes back greater to you later when you exercise godliness before others.

Thank God for men and women of God and ministries of a church that understand and operate by this ministry matrix for decision-making. Is it that important? Yes, it is!

This kind of matrix, when established and followed, will result in church health which leads to church growth. Relationships are lost on this altar more times than you can imagine. It is senseless, even satanic.

We need to take the high road. If we desire the anointing of God upon our own lives as ministers and upon our church, we cannot sacrifice it on the altar of decision-making. One day, when it is all said and done, many of these things will really not matter at all.

You can go through the proper decision-making grid in life and have both positive and negative outcomes. Of course, we love the ones that end in the positive column. It is difficult to talk about the ones that conclude in the negative column.

When I walked through my first 40-day time of fasting and prayer, that was a decision that was not easy to make nor a decision understood easily by others when I was forced to explain. A few misunderstood it, but most were intrigued by it. In 1995, this was not regarded in the norm of the Christian life nor in the life of the leader. Yet, the result was God-sized. The work of Christ within me was revolutionary. The work of Christ through our church was God-sized. To this day, the work of Christ through my life and our church is a result of that decision to enter those days in fasting and praying. Without question, it was a defining moment for all those connected to me and this ministry.

At the same time, I have gone through the exact spiritual grid and been convinced something is right under God, but the outcome would be credited to the negative column. Was the decision right? Yes. Just because you do what God wants you to do, it does not mean you will always win or succeed. Remember, *obedience is greater than sacrifice*. At times, the sacrifice may be your obedience.

When I wrote the book *The Gay Agenda*, I did it with the right heart, at the right time, and in the right way. Yet in spite of those things being done right, I am criticized to this day for standing in favor of the biblical model of marriage between a man and a woman. The book served as a spiritual and moral compass at a time in this culture when even the church cannot navigate its way with clarity. While a few may have desired for me not to have spoken to the issue, I wrote the book holding the truth of God in one hand and the love of God in the other hand. It was written with compassion, after much sacrificial research and study. Compassion reigned in the book, sharing about how our own church ministers to those struggling in the gay lifestyle. I believe that what we discerned God led us to do was credited by God and His people who love the Bible and all people as positive, but to a few it has been regarded as negative.

What is the lesson you learn from this? You can do what God wants, when God wants it, and in the way God wants it, but the result may not always be perceived as positive by people. In fact, read the 11th chapter of Hebrews again or look at the life of Paul, or even Jesus himself. As a minister, remember, your audience is one . . . God himself. More than anything in life, we want to be in His positive column. The outcomes are in His hands.

Remember: *"Trust in the LORD with all your heart, and do not rely on your own understanding; think about Him in all your ways, and He will guide you on the right paths"* (Prov. 3:5–6).

9

BALANCE
DRAWS MASSES

WE ARE LIVING IN ONE OF THE most phenomenal times in the history of the church. With technology advancing by the minute and forcing change by the hour, the church is experiencing a new day. With the dawning of this new day, opportunities exceed our imaginations. By noon, the tension rises between realism and opportunities. When the sun sets, the problems may eclipse the opportunities.

I believe you want to make a difference with your life. Whatever the ministry is you now serve, you once began with a fresh fire burning in your heart. As ministry opportunities were envisioned and some embraced, it seems that everything was not always as it appeared to be. What happened?

I can tell you what has happened to me throughout the years. My passion has gotten me in trouble more times than I can even know. When you run fast in life, it is easy to outrun the people you are called to serve and lead. I have chased innovation down many roads, even to the expense of sound judgment and theology. Ideas I thought would reach, touch, and minister to more people have cost me periodically. Why?

Passion that is unrestrained leads to extremes. Extremes may appear as creative innovations. These extremes are not always dangerous, but they can become dangerous. I have never gotten close to falling off of a cliff theologically, ecclesiologically, or pragmatically. However, I have certainly had moments in my ministry where I started toward the cliff. Honestly, you probably have as well.

As I write these words, I ask myself: "Ronnie, are you losing your edge? Are you becoming fearful of taking risks?" I think the answer to both of these questions is NO. Yet my drive to make a difference has been seasoned with learning, experience, and spiritual maturity.

For years, I have been propagating balance with everyone. I believe the limited population in my region has forced me to be a church centrist. I have had to operate with a strong element of balance with an edge in sensible innovation. At the same time, I am a risk taker and will push the envelope continuously.

Our regional population is 365,000 people, and is now growing at an accelerated rate. Yet we are not Los Angeles, Dallas, or Orlando. We never will be.

When you are doing ministry in a city with a million or more people, you can afford to operate in extremes more effectively than I can in our region. Your market reach potential is greater than mine; therefore, the ability even exists to create a niche market. I have often wondered how some large ministries in the mega-markets of the world would do in Northwest Arkansas. Simultaneously, I have wondered more how large our church might become in these same mega-markets of the world. All of this is just preacher poppycock, and I know it. We each have a unique call on how and where we are to use our giftedness to fulfill the mandate to reach our region, our nation, and our world with the good news of Jesus Christ.

Regardless of the size of your market, I am convinced that balance is essential in the long haul of church life. We do not know what the long-term success will be with so many today that are doing creative ministry successfully as they have obviously dialed into their culture effectively. I pray all of us are successful in fulfilling our unique calls from God to penetrate the world with the gospel.

My goal is not to critique or evaluate others and what they are doing. My goal in this specific chapter is to remind you of something I believe is biblical and right. Do not

> WE EACH HAVE A UNIQUE CALL ON HOW AND WHERE WE ARE TO USE OUR GIFTEDNESS TO FULFILL THE MANDATE TO REACH OUR REGION, OUR NATION, AND OUR WORLD WITH THE GOOD NEWS OF JESUS CHRIST.

mistake my belief as being non-innovative or unwilling to risk or go to the edge. If you believe that, you know little to nothing about who I am and what we do.

Listen, we were singing praise choruses before they were cool. We had screens for image magnification and videos early on in the process. We were a church without walls via our missions ministry before anyone talked much about it at all. We built the first animated children's worship building. In fact, I was able to lead to Christ the very man who has now taken what he did with our children's building years ago and expanded and improved it in some of the greatest churches in the world. We became one of the very first churches with an additional site, formalizing our identity as being "One Church in Two Locations." We will not stop here. We believe in reinventing and innovation.

I do not say all of this to boast about who we are or what we have done. We are nothing apart from Jesus and we know it. We also know we should have done, could do, and need to do so much more. I just want you to understand that in all of this and more, I have learned a great lesson I think every minister needs to know. Here is the lesson that will save you some grief and embarrassment and I believe will ensure long-term health and growth in your church regardless of its location.

SINCE THIS IS THE MESSAGE FOR THE ENTIRE WORLD, STAY CENTERED ON THE CROSS AND RESURRECTION OF JESUS CHRIST IN YOUR MESSAGE. THIS IS THE ONLY POWER OF GOD THAT IS FOR SALVATION.

Balance draws masses. When the proper balance exists in all areas of ministry, you are able to reach more people. When you are seduced into extremes, it will eventually cost you. It may cost you anointing from God, influence upon Christianity in the world, and even people who may really need the ministry of your church.

WHY BALANCE IS IMPORTANT

Reaching greater numbers of people should not be your only motivation for balance. Yes, for the long haul of church life, I believe it will help you reach more people. However, balance is important for more reasons than this.

Stay Centered on the Cross and
Resurrection in the Message

Balance is portrayed and marketed with a message that stays centered on the cross and resurrection of Jesus Christ. Even though this may be the intent of your heart, balance calls you to stay centered on the most essential of all essentials. Jesus died on the cross for the sins of the world. Jesus was raised bodily from the dead miraculously.

The only way for anyone to ever meet God is for them to personally embrace what Jesus did for them, trusting in His death and resurrection for the forgiveness of their sins. When this occurs, their sins are forgiven, Jesus comes to live within them through the person of the Holy Spirit, and they experience eternal life in heaven when they die.

Since this is the message for the entire world, stay centered on the cross and resurrection of Jesus Christ in your message. This is the only power of God that is for salvation.

All of the theological clutter in the world, as well as the temptation to out-create your last brilliant moment of creativity, may cause you to shift from the centrality of this message. Staying centered on the cross and resurrection of Jesus in your message will help you be balanced.

Stay Focused on the Great Commission

I am convinced that staying focused on the task of sharing this wonderful message of good news about Jesus around the world will help you be balanced in your life and ministry. This wonderful message of salvation was mandated by Jesus for us to share internationally and continuously. This is why we call it the Great Commission.

Sharing this message is our task. It is our commission. It is great. We cannot stop sharing it until we finish the task. We are called to make disciples around the world. This demonstrates a commitment to balance. Out of all the things you will be called upon to do in 21st century church life, ensure you do this. If not, you will chase extremes.

Keep your focus on this commission that is so great. Stay focused on it in your region. Stay focused on how to fulfill it in America. Stay focused on finishing the task globally. Stay focused.

Stay Simple by Building a Jesus Church

In the model-craze of church today, do it God's way. In this highly technological moment we are in, keep it simple. How? Be concerned in your life and ministry to build a Jesus church.

A Jesus church is not a new denomination I am creating. A Jesus church is a New Testament church. It's the kind of church you read about in the Book of Acts and the successive books of the New Testament.

A Jesus church is centered on the cross and resurrection of Jesus and is very focused on taking the message of salvation globally. A Jesus church is balanced due to its commitment to all of Scripture and is empowered by the Holy Spirit of God who is able to do the supernatural.

You may or may not be identified with a denomination. You may be identified with a certain kind of model in church life. Regardless of your status on either thing, above all, build a Jesus church. If you do not have your church so simple that you understand it is all about Jesus, you are too complicated. Balance prevails and draws masses when you become a Jesus church.

WHAT BATTLES BALANCE

Balance is always battled by an ideology or an individual who tips the scales. I like mavericks because I have learned to work with them. I like innovation because I have learned how to restrain it reasonably. However, each minister needs to know which things battle balance in church culture.

Poor Theology

When biblical illiteracy is raging from the seats of the church due to the lack of biblical teaching and preaching from the pulpits of the church, the result will be poor theology. Additionally, truth is determined in our culture by what people see, hear, feel, or experience. When you blend poor theology with the pseudo-spirituality of our day, the end result will be an impotent church. While crowds may gather to experience the most recent phenomenon, we must never equate genuine spirituality with the response of that audience.

This kind of "shake-n-bake spirituality" that is being served weekly through "church potpourri" is an indictment on the church and our commitment to biblical theology. We need to repent. We need to

> NICHE ELITISM AS A CHURCH, OR WITHIN ANY MINISTRY OF A CHURCH, WILL CAUSE IMBALANCE OVER TIME. THIS IMBALANCE WILL PROVE TO BE UNHEALTHY.

return to teaching and preaching the Bible and the whole counsel of God in a convictional, authoritative, and personal way that will engage the audience to the point that the entire church experiences the power of God. If we do not do this, poor theology will battle balance, tipping the scales toward error.

Niche Elitism

Marketing the church toward reaching a specific audience has assisted us in being somewhat successful in the short term of life. Many churches pride themselves on the kind of people they are reaching due to this strategy. They declare their niche and go after it. If they are successful by their own gauge, they can develop a spirit of elitism.

Is this New Testament? Can you find this marketing strategy in the New Testament? Perhaps you can and if so, I am glad. Niche elitism as a church, or within any ministry of a church, will cause imbalance over time. This imbalance will prove to be unhealthy.

Worship Extremes

Both poor theology and niche elitism have contributed to worship extremes. These worship extremes may occur as we try to find something for everyone or may exist because we are chasing the winds of a certain style of music. This simple point could dominate the pages of an entire book.

Whether the substance is weak in worship music or the styles are highly defined, both will limit the masses from engaging in genuine worship. Genuine worship is an encounter with Christ that results in lifestyle change.

Balance in worship is critical. When it does not exist, you had better pray you are attempting to do church in one of the great mega-cities of the world. Yet even if you have a huge population base to reach, nothing will limit the percentage of the possible pie for ministry reach in your region any quicker than extremes in worship.

HOW TO MAINTAIN BALANCE

I do believe that balance draws masses. I also believe that when fountains of explosive growth occur, the test for success will be over time. If God is in it, it will last. If it is not of God, it will not. I pray it all lasts if it is Bible-based, Jesus-centered, and Holy Spirit-controlled. It is incumbent on ministers to think about balance and how to maintain it in churches across the world.

Based on the Bible

If your church is not based on the Bible, balance will not occur. If you do not read it, teach it, preach it, and live it, balance will not occur.

The only equalizing source of authority in this world is the Bible, the precious Word of God. It has stood the test of time.

It is God's truth for today. It is the way you and your church can stay balanced.

Heart for all people

I believe the church should cross generational, racial, and socio-economic lines. The only way to have a heart for all people is to minister to and reach people from all walks of life. When a church does not do this, they will forget many of the people in their community in the name of "our niche" and "our style." Over the course of time, this will be very unhealthy. Having a heart for all people will result in balance in your ministry and church.

Listen to wise, godly counsel

When a minister is headstrong about "his way of doing church" and it becomes "the only way," he develops arrogance. Arrogance puts the entire church in jeopardy. This is why each minister needs to learn to be a listener.

Listen to wise and godly counsel. This may come from other ministers on the team, from across the country, or from some lay person in the church. If they are wise and godly, learn to listen to them when you hear them singing the same song, calling for you to have greater balance in your ministry and church. God may be saying something to you through them.

A FRESH CALL

I am compelled by the Lord to issue you a fresh call. This fresh call to ministers and churches is something I have done for the past several years. It is what the American church needs to hear and do and the unchurched culture needs to see. Here is the fresh call to each of you and the need of the day: *Practice orthodoxy packaged in innovation.*

I believe strongly that real truth and doctrine can be packaged in innovation. I believe orthodoxy is not threatened by innovation because it is truth. Truth always lasts. I believe innovative methodology needs genuine substance. Jesus packaged His truth in a way that people in His day understood, using innovation to do it. The New Testament church echoed this uniqueness.

In 21st century church life, we have some ministers and churches entrenched with the purity of their truth, ignoring the power of innovation. On the other hand, we have ministers and churches that are as cutting edge as Las Vegas or Hollywood technology, but doctrinally are as shallow as an inch. Each of the groups has "stand offs," exercising their spiritual gift of criticism toward each other. Neither is right and neither honors God. Both mislead people about true Christianity.

I believe the unchurched and the church will run toward a minister and a church that will practice orthodoxy packaged in innovation. At the least, the world will give you more credibility. More importantly, I believe you will represent the heart of Jesus' truth, life, and ministry when you practice orthodoxy packaged in innovation.

When this occurs in the right way with the right spirit, this kind of balance will draw masses of people.

Remember: *"As for Me, if I am lifted up from the earth I will draw all people to Myself"* (John 12:32).

10

How to Believe God for Your Future

I WAS VERY ANXIOUS FOR GOD to place me in my first full-time church while I was in seminary. After I had preached at a particular church in the Dallas-Fort Worth region under consideration to be their next pastor, Jeana and I would drive by there and think about what I would do if they would just call me to serve them. On the nights we did not drive by there, we would sit on the front porch awaiting their phone call. Hours stretched into days and days into weeks. Obviously, we did not end up going to this specific pastorate. I am still waiting for their call!

Even though I had served one church on the weekends as their pastor, I was so naive. It is embarrassing to think how we would jump any time the phone would ring, hoping it was the church we had preached in weeks before.

This journey was the first time I remember having to come through the process and just believe God. It has been repeated numerous times since those seminary days. The mystery of the future still entices me to this day.

The future is something we want to know, yet is impossible to know. Nothing can cause more stress and distress than thinking about the future and its relationship to you. As a minister, you can become plagued by worry to the point that you become pitiful by your discontentment. This is not God's will for you or your ministry.

I have had to go back in my mind so many times to that dormitory room in the spring of my freshman year at college where the Lord gave me a powerful word for my future. In Psalm 75:6–7 it says:

> Exaltation does not come from the east, the west, or the desert, for God is the judge: He brings down one and exalts another.

On that spring afternoon, I became convinced that God had an enormous plan for my life. What I needed to do was just believe God for my future.

As I have matured in life and in my walk with Christ, I have had to review those verses hundreds of times. Those life verses have held my hands in guidance and supported my knees in prayer. Is it easier now when decisions about the future arise? Not really. Yes, I do have a little history to think about what God has done and how He has worked in my life. However, it still comes back to the excruciating process of prayer over the process of time.

The great news that I have learned through experience is that when God chooses not to do something I thought He would do, it is for protection on my life. I was not very good at understanding this in the first phase of my ministry. When things did not go my way, I would feel rejected and discouraged. Today, I feel protected and loved! I feel that because I have learned to believe God for my future. How can you believe God for your future? You need to know these five things.

KNOW WHAT GOD IS SAYING TO YOU

As I write this chapter, I am completing a painful prayer process pertaining to a huge opportunity in my life. It is an opportunity that has future written all over it. I have had to pray like never before, receive counsel from men I know and do not know, and live with what God has spoken to me for several weeks before it is confirmed

> THE GREAT NEWS THAT I HAVE LEARNED THROUGH EXPERIENCE IS THAT WHEN GOD CHOOSES NOT TO DO SOMETHING I THOUGHT HE WOULD DO, IT IS FOR PROTECTION ON MY LIFE.

or rejected. What I do know with confidence, even though the final outcome is God's decision, is that I am doing what I believe God wants me to do at this time.

How do I know that? The Bible is the constant source from which I draw wells of insight. Each time I sense that God speaks, I mark the item in my Bible and date the experience. Additionally, I write down in my prayer journal what God has said and is saying to me about this futuristic possibility. I share it with few to none and then put it on my points to pray about daily.

Once God speaks through the Word, I pray. In that prayer process, I exercise the practice of believing God for my future. I stand on His authority, the Word of God, and declare what God is saying to me. This builds my faith like nothing else. As you pray, ask God for His protection on your desire to please Him. He has protected me many times and He will protect you.

Therefore, it is essential to know what God is saying to you through His Word. He is speaking. Are you listening? You can only believe God when you know what He is saying to you.

KNOW YOURSELF WELL

Each of you has been endowed with gifts from the Holy Spirit. Each of you has been called to express those gifts through a specific calling in ministry. God does not ignore the giftedness He has placed in you when He places His leadership upon your future. He will never lead you to do what He has not equipped you to do.

He may use a new calling or a renewed calling to refine you, develop you, or mature you. He knows your gifts, but He also knows all of His intentions for you when He created you. He realizes what your potential is in Him.

How well do you know yourself? Do you know your spiritual gifts? Have you re-evaluated that recently? How have you developed other skills in your life that may be what you might categorize as a spiritual gift? What are you passionate about right now? Has God been putting some new desires in your heart over the course of the last few weeks, months, or years? Have you revisited your initial calling and even the initial years after it, to consider what He put in your heart in those early years? When is the last time something deeply spiritual occurred in you, altering you and perhaps even your future or desires? What do you want to do with the rest of your life?

> **KNOW YOURSELF WELL. WHEN YOU DO, YOU ARE SETTING YOURSELF UP TO BELIEVE GOD IN A MORE PRODUCTIVE WAY CONCERNING YOUR FUTURE.**

I believe there comes a time when we get very secure in who we are and what God has gifted us to be in life. We cease or at least restrain our aspirations, realizing the unique gift mixture within us and the unique calling to us. Are you there? Try to get to this place.

The water becomes very cloudy concerning our future until we know who we really are in life and ministry. Until this happens, we imagine ourselves to be in places we have no business being or doing things we are not really gifted or called to do. At this point, discontentment sets in about what we are doing and where we are doing it, further muddying the already cloudy water as we look toward our future. This is not God's will for any of us.

Re-evaluate who you are right now. Re-introduce yourself to you. There is a new you that sets in through maturity and development. Know yourself well. When you do, you are setting yourself up to believe God in a more productive way concerning your future.

KNOW YOUR MISSION AND PURPOSE

I went through this process extensively this past year. God rattled my life with possibilities last year concerning my future. There was a time when so many things were possibilities, it appeared strongly that transition was about to take place. I was not looking for any of it to occur and I had initiated none of it, which made it even more frightening, but exciting. However, one by one, God took care of each one. I am still here in Northwest Arkansas. It was a tremendous experience for me to walk through because I felt so loved and protected by God. I have no regrets pertaining to my conduct or response to what God brought my way for discussion and consideration. It was a very healthy experience. As a minister, it is also a great blessing to know that God knows your cell phone number and e-mail address.

These experiences which began in February and ended by the late summer, as well as my dad's death just before Thanksgiving, moved me into a process of re-evaluating a lot of things about me, my church, my giftedness, my passions, my desires for my future, and, most of all, what needed to be my new or revised mission and purpose for the rest of my life.

Therefore, from Thanksgiving until just after the first of the year, I walked through this process. I got to know me again. I stopped long enough to evaluate my development in various areas. I did this with prayer from my lips, a pen in one hand, and a Bible in the other hand. I talked to God. I listened to God speak to me from His Word. I wrote in my prayer journal.

On January 4, 2006, it all came together. I began to write, based on what God had placed on my heart through the reading of Scripture. The following has become my new mission and purpose in life:

> *My mission and purpose in life is to use my gifts, leadership, influence, and resources to take the good news of Jesus Christ to the entire world.*

From this statement, I began to write down four major areas I believed the Lord had placed on my heart about how He wanted me to accomplish my mission and purpose. In fact, under each of the four major areas, there is some detail about each one.

Daily, I pray through this one page document. It helps keep fresh on my mind what I am about in life. It also creates a level of accountability for me. This is my vision path.

All of this is future driven and I believe God for it daily. So much would have never occurred without the supernatural element intervening through it. I am amazed and astounded, even extremely humbled, by God's activity since that time toward the initial fulfillment of some God-sized matters. What God does is His determination. My role is to believe God for my future.

You can do this too. You need to know what God is saying to you. You need to know yourself well. You need to know your mission and purpose in life. Remember, God wants to use you in a maximum way to expand His kingdom throughout the ends of the world. In order for Him to do that, all of this is part of the process spiritually. Enjoy the journey.

KNOW THE RIGHT QUESTIONS TO ASK

When you follow the process I have written about in this chapter, the Lord may begin to bring some opportunities your way. They may or may not mean a geographical transition, but perhaps a transition in you or the ministry you serve. These opportunities may exist right now. I would counsel you to stop long enough to go through what I have stated in this chapter thus far. Then I believe it is important to consider asking yourself some hard questions. In fact, whatever kind of transition you face personally or in ministry, geographically or internally, these are good questions and right questions to ask yourself. These are some decision-making questions.

Q 1: Did this opportunity begin with God?

Is God originating this, or did you begin it due to your interest in it? Is this you or God? First Thessalonians 5:24 says, *"He who calls you is faithful, who also will do it."*

If there is something clicking here, if God is calling you, He will do it. No one can stop the hand of God from working in your life.

Q 2: Am I willing to do it?

Am I willing to walk away from this as much as I am willing to do it? God wants you to be willing to do anything, anywhere, at anytime. You need to be as willing to stay as you are to leave. I believe God searches for a willing heart before He makes His will clear. Again, never forget: God wants you to be willing to do anything, anywhere, at anytime.

Q 3: Is it God's timing?

Just because something may come your way and you are willing to do it, it may not be God's exact timing. He may want you to do it, but just not now, perhaps later.

At the same time, there are times when God brings something that makes you wonder, "Does God not realize this is poor timing?" God's timing is not by your timetable or even your church's timetable. God does not live by your watch or calendar, but by seasons and moments. This may be His moment to express himself through you and your ministry. Whatever will bring Him the most glory is what it is all about anyway.

Q 4: Is God saying anything to me through James 3:13–18?

I will let you read this biblical account, but it is a very pivotal revelation concerning wisdom. James shows us the difference in wisdom that comes from the world and wisdom that comes from God. Wisdom is critical in all decision-making.

Human wisdom has the components of bitter envy, self-justification, evil possibilities, earthly or fleshly activity, confusion, is self-seeking, unspiritual, and can even be ignited by the demonic. I realize this is strong, but so much stuff we do in the name of being "spiritual" is very carnal and fleshly.

Conversely, God's wisdom has the components of purity, a willingness to yield, no hypocrisy, is full of good fruits, is gentle, merciful, peaceful, and unwavering. This is strong and can be quite confirming for you.

Go through the text yourself. Ensure that human wisdom is not more existent than God's wisdom pertaining to your situation. This text may rule out this new opportunity for your future or it may become your cheerleader as a confirmation. Learn to make decisions based off of God's Word.

Q 5: Does this decision demonstrate the fruit of the Holy Spirit?

Read Galatians 5:22–23 which gives the account of the fruit of the Holy Spirit. After you read it initially, ask yourself about each one of the fruits, "How is the _____ factor?" Place each of the fruits in the blank one at a time.

Q 6: Does this decision bring glory to God?

I believe each decision you make is to bring glory to God. This is not about you, so please remember this as you consider your future.

Q 7: What is God saying to me?

After working through these questions and others, be honest and answer this seventh question, "What is God saying to me?" I believe there are times when the Lord lets you have the privilege of choosing between two great options for your life. He looks at you and says, "You have worked through this. Your heart is pure. Do what you want to do." He is your Father and you are His child. Just as you do with your children at times, God may choose to do this with you. Just ensure your decision is God's best for you. He is into using you up to the maximum for the greatest glory unto himself alone.

By the way, always follow this as well: *When in doubt, don't!* Do not force something that is not right. Wait until you know, even though there will usually be an element of faith involved.

These are the right questions to ask yourself when you are facing some kind of transition.

As we move to closure, remember, I have talked to you about the importance of knowing what God is saying to you. I have encouraged you to know yourself well. I have highlighted the importance of knowing your mission and purpose in life and ministry. I have just given you the right questions to ask yourself when facing some kind of transition. All of these and more are very important to help you know how to believe God for your future. However, there is a final statement I want you to bank your life, family, and ministry upon.

KNOW THAT YOU CAN BELIEVE GOD

When Paul was in the uncertain waters recorded in Acts 27, he declared to those on the storm-tossed boat, "Take courage . . . I believe God!" Life and ministry are full of uncertainty. Doing God's work may result in pain, loss, suffering, discouragement, and even, sometimes, death. This is why you need courage and faith in all matters in life. In order to be a minister who operates by faith, you are going to have to exercise courage and belief in God daily. People do not follow unclear and uncertain leaders. They yearn for clarity and confidence from you.

You can do this because you know who you have faith in as you live life and ministry. You are not trusting in yourself, but in God. Paul declared to his young preacher protégé, Timothy, some words every minister needs to have in his heart. He stated these words:

> . . . *I know whom I have believed and am persuaded that He is able to guard what has been entrusted to me until that day* (2 Tim. 1:12).

Discontentedness and discouragement in ministry can be avoided and overcome when you live life and ministry believing God.

If we were sitting in a Starbucks conversing over a cup of coffee, discussing all the matters I have shared with you in this chapter, I would look at you at this time and say, "Sooner or later, you are just going to have to believe God." It really comes down to believing God for your future. How do I know this?

MY FINAL WORDS TO YOU

I want to close this chapter and book with a couple of thoughts for your consideration. Since ministry is so much about the future and preparing to engage it, it is essential that each minister know they can believe God for their future.

I know you can believe God for your future because you can trust God and His Word. His character is impeccable and He always stands by His Word. My friend, dear minister, believe God. Do not trust yourself, another minister, a new method, or a creative tool. Trust God himself and His Word for your future life and ministry. You can trust Him.

I know you can believe God for your future because I have experienced His guidance and protection through 30 years of pastoral ministry. Thank God I am where I am and doing what I am doing. If I had gone to so many places I have imagined myself to be or done whatever it is I have imagined myself to do, I would not be in the center of the will of God and my success would have been limited or none. Thank God, He protects me when I do not know how to protect myself.

> I KNOW YOU CAN BELIEVE GOD FOR YOUR FUTURE BECAUSE I HAVE EXPERIENCED HIS GUIDANCE AND PROTECTION THROUGH 30 YEARS OF PASTORAL MINISTRY.

God knows what is best for you 24/7, every day of your life and ministry. Remember, He designed you. Do not forget that. He has a purpose for you. He has a will and intention for you. From the womb of your mother, He formulated a role for you in life and ministry.

Pray for His guidance to be as clear as the sun. Pray for His protection to guard you on every side. I am so thankful God has done this with me for these 30 years of pastoral moments, of which 20 of those years have been in one church located in Northwest Arkansas.

One of the greatest privileges you have in life is be one of God's ministers. There are many things you need to know, but above all, you must know you can trust Him.

When you trust Him, you will learn this one thing about ministry: There is nothing like it in the world.

Remember: *"I rise before dawn and cry out for help; I put my hope in Your word"* (Ps. 119:147).

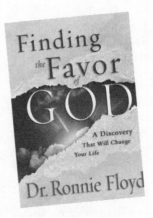